GARY DOHERTY

MINDSET OF AN ENTREPRENEUR

From a young age I always felt different – different to most people. Or at least in my mind I felt I was. I knew I had something more to offer the world than what school, parents or society traditionally teaches us. I believe, looking back, this was my entrepreneurial spirit that I was born with. This is an age-old debate, I know. Are entrepreneurs born or bred? I believe true entrepreneurs are born and they always come to the surface at some point in their life.

What happens with many people is that they permanently become a product of their environment and settle for the status quo. That is also fine.

That said, that was never me. I could never settle for the norm. Always because I felt I wasn't normal. When I was younger, that had negative connotations, but from about the age of twenty-four up to now, forty-five, it is one of my superpowers. I believe we all have our own superpower.

My mindset has greatly evolved. Some characteristics of myself that have been highlighted to me in a few 360-degree feedback sessions were: my drive, determination, relentlessness, resilience and the ability to keep going no matter what, no matter when, no matter how.

I feel this is crucial as an entrepreneur as the road travelled is seldom smooth. Expect and embrace setbacks, knockbacks and temporary failure. Failure or *perceived* failure is one of the true keys to success. Fail forward; and that leads me to my last point on how my mindset has truly evolved.

I realise all the above are crucial to my success, but I would now add *continuous improvement* mindset to that.

Continuous improvement as part of your mindset is crucial, I believe. I'd go as far as saying critical. You can be hardworking, but if you are doing the wrong things or not doing enough of the right things, you are only practising a failed process and won't make the strides you should and could.

To improve takes mental fortitude as you have to accept many mistakes in your own self. You must be open to change, open to constructive critique. From my experience this where a lot of people fail. They want to hear the good but not the bad. It can be hard to hear, but put ego aside, get aligned to your why and relentlessly improve.

PERSONAL DEVELOPMENT JOURNEY

My personal development journey began consciously as an adult at around thirty years of age. For me, it came with maturity and with my inquisitive mindset. I have always wondered how things could be done better, could I do more and how. I would read around subjects I was interested in, and I began listening to TED Talks which would inspire me years later to become a two-time TED speaker and multiple-time TED curator and licence holder. What I would learn, as this attitude and mindset took me into the personal development world, is that I was already practising a lot of the things I would later go on to study. I was what is known as an *unconscious competent*. When you are unconsciously doing the right thing but aren't thinking about the process or the rationale behind it, it comes naturally. The problem with that is when you are having an off day, you don't have the conscious ability to go to your personal development toolkit to address it and turn it around.

My passion for lifelong learning naturally took me right into the heart of personal development. I realised early on in my journey the value of having a mentor or mentors to advise, direct, guide and hold you accountable. I realised the value of reading the correct material from credible sources; filling my brain with knowledge. This increased my confidence.

One of the best books I have ever read and that had the biggest impact on me was *Think and Grow Rich* by Napoleon Hill. In fact, I've read it eight times! Always learning and always improving!

Today I run THINK Network Europe's largest independent network where we provide environments for individuals to be the best versions of themselves. So, for me, my personal development has truly evolved. From being an individual who immersed myself into the world for my own personal benefit, I now help the masses enjoy the same journey.

BUSINESS ADVICE

My first taste of business was in 2006. Cast your mind back to the property boom. My entrepreneurial spirit spotted opportunities and I took them. I built a large property portfolio over three years, turning over millions of pounds – then lost it all! My entrepreneurial spirit led me back into business with THINK Network in 2018 and we have grown to be a proud six-figure business.

My top twelve tips in business are:

1. Do not think you know everything. You don't. In fact, you may be the visionary in your business, but you should have people much better or more capable than you in key positions around you. This is one of the keys to growth. Think you know it all and you know nothing; think you know very little and you can learn a lot.
2. Ego. Don't develop one or let one get in your way. When you are doing well, or very well, don't get too high or think you've made it. This, in fact, is a good time to improve again. Having a humble but confident mindset in business will serve you well.

3. Be financially astute. Have a *rainy day* fund. Don't think that money is going to be plentiful all the time. Great if it is, but make sure you're prepared for if it's not.

4. Keep your overheads lean. Ask yourself when you are contemplating making considerable purchases, *Do I need it or do I just want it?*

5. Look for efficient ways of doing business – can you do something virtually that speeds the process up?

6. Omnipresence. If you are selling a product or service, you need to be visible on social media. It is a modern crime in business to avoid this.

7. Be niche with your offering. You cannot be all things to all people. Find your niche and become world-class.

8. If you are looking to grow from a six-figure business to a seven-figure business, you need systems, processes, automation, and smart lead-generation, sales and marketing strategies.

9. Collaboration. Be more than open to working with other people – seek it. We can always do more together.

10. Consider joint ventures. Teaming up with complimentary products or services is one of the quickest ways to scale.

11. Integrity. Nothing ever good came from doing the wrong thing.

12. Values. Know your values and don't comprise from what you believe to be morally right.

OVERCOMING ADVERSITY

The word *resilience* screams out at me when I think of overcoming adversity. Being resilient is the ability to bounce back and bounce back quickly. Again, this divides opinion on whether you

THINK NETWORK

Levelling Up⇧

Mindset Hacks of Trailblazing Entrepreneurs

Typeset in Sabon LT Pro 11/15pt

A catalogue record for this
work is available from the
National Library of Australia

National Library of Australia Catalogue-in-Publication data:
Levelling Up/Think Network

ISBN:
978-0-6454076-1-7
(Paperback)

ISBN:
978-0-6454076-2-4
(Ebook)

CONTENTS

are born with it, or if it can be developed. My personal belief is both.

From my experience, I originally was able to overcome adversity by leaning on and borrowing the belief someone else had in me.

What do I mean? I had someone in my life who told me they believed in me – even when *I* didn't. So, when I faced adversity, I leaned on that borrowed belief, and told myself I had the ability to overcome it. That I was good enough and I had the ability to keep going and improve. This self-talk is crucial to overcoming adversity.

Now, being a conscious competent, I can go to this personal development toolkit and affirm this to myself whenever I need to. Affirmations played a key role in the development of my resilience, which enabled me to overcome any adversity I faced.

I have faced losing a business, a property portfolio, my own home and vehicles, and have rebuilt it all; I have faced adversity in the form of losing loved ones.

I should add that I am a man of faith. Leaning on my faith has brought me through adversity and it would be amiss of me not to acknowledge that in this book.

Having a close inner circle and strong loving marriage has always been to my advantage also in overcoming any adversity I have ever faced.

GOALS & GOAL SETTING

Goals are a crucial part of achieving success. Without them I believe you are going forward aimlessly. In Napoleon Hill's *Think and Grow Rich* he tells us we are goal-striving mechanisms in perpetual and forever increase.

In short, we should always be moving forward with goals.

My goals are in three categories: Type A, B and C

TYPE A GOAL

This is a goal that you possibly have been procrastinating but you know exactly how to achieve. Not only do you know how to achieve it, but you know how much it costs, how long it will take – you just have to take action.

For example, it could be that your type A goal is, *I am going to walk thirty minutes per day for thirty days*. You simply do it and you achieve it.

TYPE B GOAL

This is a goal you have a fair idea you can achieve somehow, someway. It is a goal that stretches you mentally, and you know you are going to have to figure out the best way to achieve it. You may have to take advice, or search for information to achieve this particular goal. But ultimately you know you can do it.

For example, your type B goal could be that you want to get fit enough to run a marathon. For this, you may need to join a running club, hire a personal trainer, invest in proper training gear and build yourself up under the guidance of an expert until you are ready to achieve this result and achieve your type B goal.

TYPE C GOAL

These are the scary, outrageous goals. The ones you only dream about, and some may call fantasy goals. These are goals that sound a little crazy when you say them out loud. Achieving a type C goal requires a higher level of thinking and mindset growth. You must be vibrating at a level that leads you to do extraordinary things to make extraordinary things happen. It requires attributes such as faith, belief, knowing and courage.

An example of a type C goal could be you want to do three TED Talks when you have no prior public speaking experience, and the thought terrifies you!

TOP TIPS

1. Be authentic. Be yourself, as everyone else is taken. Be proud to be you, accept yourself – flaws and all. You are perfectly imperfect and that is perfect! When you are being yourself, it frees you to express yourself with confidence and courage. Be authentic.

2. Know your circle. Know who you can go to for advice, opinions, feedback, support and encouragement. Keep that circle small and serve them with your heart and soul. Outside your immediate family, I recommend a good mastermind group.

3. Serving mentality. Think about what you can do for others as opposed to what you can get. Do this with boundaries. Only serve those who will benefit from your kindness and support. This mentality has served me well as I have received support back tenfold.

4. Be financially astute. I have realised the importance of saving, investing, building a good credit rating, creating multiple sources of income and not spending foolishly. Money itself doesn't make you happy, in my opinion, but it gives you choices that can create freedom that can bring you happiness.

5. Self-belief. When levelling up, it is vital to believe. Know that doubt is perfectly normal. You will experience doubt regularly. Know that everyone does, and sometimes daily. No-one, and I mean *no-one,* has it all figured out. Affirm to yourself that you believe in you, no matter what. Believe more than you doubt.

AMY DOHERTY

THE MINDSET OF AN ENTREPRENEUR

Being twenty-five years old and walking out of your nine to five job role is quite the step to take – right? That is exactly what I did in December 2020. I wasn't feeling fulfilled, I lacked passion working in the retail sector, I felt that I had to stay in the position I was in because I was a single parent and making that leap wasn't just on me, it would impact my two boys also.

My dad had started taking THINK Network to new heights, and in the background, I was his content creator – creating all his graphics and social media posts. Clients and followers noticed and soon Dad was getting messages from individuals asking who was behind the work. That is when my baby, THINK Digital, was born.

THINK Digital is my creative space. At school I was always artistic, it was my passion, and I lost myself in a world of creativity. I love seeing my imagination come to life in my work. So, in December 2020 I handed in my resignation, and I have honestly not looked back since. Sometimes we need to have that faith in ourselves which, sadly, so many of us don't. I know I didn't feel good enough, and sometimes still to this day I have imposter syndrome, where I look around me and think, *What am I doing here?* But the older I get, the more confident I am, and I know that I have what it takes to better myself and my two boys' lives. Taking that leap is where the magic happens. Feel the fear and do it anyway.

THINK Digital is where my clients come to me with their business, values, and what they have in mind to enhance that, to gain visibility – and we always make it happen. Thankfully, my clients have all believed in my creative ability and flow of working, so I have a lot of freedom and control now that I am my own boss. Being such a big part of THINK Network, and working for that business on the daily, has helped me grow and flourish. Never underestimate yourself or what you can achieve. Everyone with a strong passion can turn that into a reality if they want it badly enough and they can all achieve the *mindset of an entrepreneur*. Just take the leap. Take the chance. Magic will follow and you will wonder why you didn't do it sooner. Live the life you want. Do not wake up every day and go to a job that doesn't fulfil you. Life is so much more than that.

PERSONAL DEVELOPMENT JOURNEY

My personal development journey really started the day I gave birth to my first son, Mason. I had just turned twenty exactly a week before, and my life honestly changed for the absolute better the moment he was placed into my arms. My Granda Marshall, who was basically a second father to me, had passed away only six weeks before I gave birth. Completely out of the blue. Mason was appropriately named Mason Marshall – which my Granda knew of before he passed away. Those two major life events in quick succession made me grow up a lot and look at the bigger picture. When Mason was around eighteen months old, he still wasn't talking and was doing quirky habits like spinning himself around and around for sometimes hours at a time. I voiced my concerns to my health visitor, who quickly got Mason referred to where he needed to be. The reoccurring word was *autism*. In November 2018, Mason was diagnosed with ASD – autism spectrum disorder. During this time another three major life events happened – I gave birth to my second son Noah; my Nana, who was my best friend, and again, like a second mother to me, passed away while living at home with us; and my relationship with my boys' dad had ended for good. That is some hefty stuff, am I right? Noah is still, to this day, non-verbal and is awaiting his ASD diagnosis like his big brother.

The world of ASD has taught me so much. It has helped me become the best version of myself. I no longer ever look and judge anyone or make assumptions. I also love nothing more than using my voice for my two boys and so many others – which leads me on to my TEDx Talk. At school I was the shy girl who wouldn't so much as raise her hand (even when I knew the answer) just because I didn't want eyes on me for the fear of messing up or stumbling over my words. I was the outsider at school. I didn't ever fit in because I was so quiet, and my peers found that made me an easy target to make fun of or to pick out my flaws. I never honestly felt good enough or beautiful enough until I became a mother. That's when I really found who I was and saw myself as strong and confident. Single motherhood will do that to you.

My TEDx Talk, *My Boys Don't Have to Change, Society Does*, was to highlight the treatment of those with ASD and how they are often pushed to the side and made to conform to societal norms, but my message was this – let them embrace that amazing gift they have been given. Yes, they are different, but in the most amazing ways. The hundreds of messages I received from other ASD families, ASD individuals and others who were willing to learn and accept them made my heart burst with pride. That talk has now been viewed thousands of times and is still on the up every single day.

A couple of weeks before I delivered my TEDx Talk, Elon Musk hosted SNL and on-air declared with pride, 'I am autistic,' and went on to say, 'I am the first autistic person to host this show – but I think I am just the first to say that I am.' That struck a chord within me. How right he was. Individuals with ASD are made to feel like they shouldn't be proud of who they are – again, to conform. But no, I want Mason and Noah to stand proud and scream it from the rooftops that they ARE autistic. They are magic. They are gifts with their gift. I will always use my voice to empower not just my boys, but other individuals with ASD. My voice is my gift, as is my love as the mother of two very special little boys. Noah has made having a voice (something most of us take for granted) stand out even more to me, and until he can use his, I'll shout twice as loud for the both of us. But he will eventually use his own, and then his big brother, himself and I will come together to use our voices to make a difference in the world and to advocate for the better. I will advocate for as long as I am alive. It takes a spark to start a fire, so I will be that spark.

As we enter a new school year, Mason has a full-time assistant now and is statemented – finally! Noah is heading into his nursery year with an assistant and his statement also, something Mason did not have, but Noah was pushed up the list due to being non-verbal at present, which I am so grateful for especially after Mason's experience during his nursery year – it was not a positive one, to say the least. His nursery teacher wanted him to only do one-hour days while his peers stayed four. Mason's meltdowns increased and his emotions were all over the place. His primary school, however, have been amazing with him, and they encourage his gift and allow him to just be Mason. I owe so much to his teachers, classroom assistant and principal. Noah is attending a different nursery school, who also seem to want to embrace his gift and allow him to just be Noah. It's incredible how different outlooks and mindsets can change your whole life. As Noah walked through his nursery school doors, into a place of acceptance and love, my heart could have burst seeing him step into his next chapter as exactly who he is.

So, my personal development journey? I owe it all to my two boys. They have shown me a world that I didn't know existed, but that I am so glad I now do. It has connected me with others who are experiencing the same thing and all the milestones we can take for granted in everyday life, every little thing is a celebration now. Going to the cinema, having a haircut, getting a school photograph – all major milestones in our home and I wouldn't have it any other way. Life is so much more magical with the gift of Mason and Noah.

BUSINESS ADVICE

My business advice is from the perspective of a single mother. Firstly, it is not a weakness to ask for help. By that, I mean: don't be afraid to ask family and friends for their help and support.

Whether that is looking after the kids, helping around the house or simply showing you support on social media platforms by sharing or liking an important post – it will give you breathing space to focus further on your business and will reap rewards in the long term.

Another piece of advice that I must share is to always put your children first. Find that perfect balance between work and family. Learn that to achieve the right balance you will have to work around their timetable, i.e. school hours, bedtimes, hours visiting their dad, etc. There are resources available out there for single parents which include websites such as Enterprise Nation – on this website you can connect with like-minded single parents. The Single Mum's Business Network is also another great resource which is available to you. Most of these online resources are free, but provide invaluable support to so many, including workshops and networking events to meet in person and build your business and your brand even further.

Podcasts are a great way of killing two birds with one stone. Listening to a podcast while you drive the kids to school or do your daily chores is excellent, free and useful. For example, Janet Murray's podcast is amazing and really focuses on helping small businesses start up.

Trust your gut instinct – always do the right thing, if something feels wrong, it probably is. Having a bit of confidence and self-belief is crucial to success as you will have to weather the highs and lows by yourself. Don't get caught up in competing with other businesses. There is always enough business for everybody. Believe in yourself and set your own goals and targets – it is your confidence that will carry you through. Taking the bold step to go out on your own is hard. However, for single parents, the playing field is far from level and the challenges are always that much greater.

The key for any entrepreneur thinking of starting a business is to learn from others who have been in the same situation who can help navigate the demands of running a small business.

OVERCOMING ADVERSITY

Adversity. In the dictionary, adversity is described as a 'difficult or unpleasant situation'. Accurate if you ask me. Being a single mum to two autistic boys, it is safe to safe I face adversity daily. So much so, I have gotten pretty used to it at this point. I don't even really think about it anymore. I don't know if that is a good or a bad thing. People look at me and not only do they see a twenty-five-year-old with two sons, but they also really like to judge the fact that I am single. Why is being single so bad? We live in a society where modern families and co-parenting is becoming more and more common, yet there is still this chunk of us that frown upon someone who is 'single'. Single isn't inadequate, or lacking in something. Single, to me, is brave, strong and independent. It takes courage to walk away from something that no longer serves you. I don't see that as a difficult or unpleasant situation at all. Even though I am single, I want my boys to always view that choice as a strong one. Because of that decision,

I am a much happier, content mum to them. The last thing I would ever want is for them to witness arguing on the daily, or to see me unhappy.

Autism. Another major cause of adversity. When we are in a supermarket and Mason or Noah feels overwhelmed, we encounter the stares of others, the shaking of heads, judgement. It is not in the slightest easy to go through that. Though adverse and traumatic childhood experiences are common in the general population and strongly associated with poor physical and mental health outcomes throughout life, little is known about the prevalence and impact of these difficulties on the lives of children with ASD. Children with ASD are far more likely to develop anxiety, depression and other mental health conditions than other children. Rates of trauma-related disorders, such as post-traumtic stress disorder (PTSD), in ASD are far lower and rarely considered in autism research. Studies suggest that people with ASD may encounter a range of both obvious stressors (such as bullying, frightening medical procedures or hospitalisations) and less obvious stressors (intense sensory sensitivities, social stigma and difficulties coping with change) from a young age. This is just a tiny part of wanting to be a voice for the autistic community and helping in any way that I can to break the boundaries and change their world for the better. No-one should have to suffer or be unfairly treated just because they work differently. Who is to say that we neurotypicals aren't the ones who are the odd ones out? Yet, we are embraced for who we are because that fits into society and the so-called norms. This is not okay. It needs to change. Not just for my sons, but for the whole community. Young or old. It must stop.

I looked up the dictionary's meaning of autism and found this: 'A developmental disorder of variable severity that is characterised by difficulty in social interaction and communication and by restricted or repetitive patterns of thought and behaviour.' Really? I then looked up what the dictionary describes disorder as and found: 'A state of confusion, to disrupt the systematic functioning or neat arrangement of.' Now if that doesn't say everything you need to know, I don't know what will. To disrupt the systematic functioning. That is exactly what society does not want, what they are afraid of happening. Therefore, society likes to stick to the set norms and rules – but what if we just let everyone be as they are? I think we would have a much brighter, colourful, magical, amazing world, and who knows what could be achieved. Autism acceptance can be defined as an individual feeling accepted or appreciated as an autistic person, with autism positively recognised and accepted by others and the self as an integral part of that individual.

GOALS & GOAL SETTING

How many times this week have you been asked whether you've made any New Year's resolutions? How many times in your life have you been asked about your goals for the future? How would you answer if you had a limited concept of time and limited organisational skills? What is a goal, anyway?!

Individuals with ASD can be taught goal setting with a very small goal that can be met in seven days using the SMART method.

Specific: The goal must be clearly stated, without words such as 'more', 'longer' or 'better' because they are too vague.

Measurable: The goal should be something that can be measured so that success is clear.

Are you motivated? Traditionally, the A stands for attainable, but we prefer, 'are you motivated?' so we know why the individual wants to meet the goal.

Realistic: Is the goal something that the individual has the skills and ability to accomplish?

Timely: Can the goal be accomplished in one week?

The thing with goals is that we must understand all the rules before we play the game. This includes the rules for what happens when we do not meet a goal. **This point is vital: always offer a way to make up a missed goal!**

The six main things I focus on personally to fulfil my goals are as follows:

- Health.
- Faith.
- Work.
- Family.
- Money.
- Personal.

Lastly, goals I believe single parents should focus on are as follows:

- Review your finances.
- Review your budget.
- Save more money this year.
- Earn more this year.
- Focus on personal goals.
- Connect with your kids.
- Reconnect with old friends, family or find your tribe.

You have such a big job as a single mother. It probably isn't what you signed up for, but it can be an amazing joy and strength. Your child will learn a level of empathy, appreciation and work ethic that many other kids won't have. The bond between a child and single mother is often supportive and unwavering. And that's okay!

The key is to remain the pillar of strength that you and your child needs. Use these goals to cope with the extra stress and overwhelm that are part of the deal. Get your finances in order, then make sure you have enough time to focus on your personal goals. Make time to find your stress relief and happiness. Build and nurture your relationships. Find your tribe if you don't have family and friends that can really relate to your struggles.

Most importantly, focus on your goals so that you have the patience and inner joy to connect with your kids. You don't get to take back time. The last thing you want is to look back and realise that you didn't spend enough quality time with your child.

ACTION STEPS

- Review your finances, either by tracking your finances or use an app to do most of the work for you.
- Establish or review your budget. Find ways to adjust your budget to save more money.
- Brainstorm ways to earn more money. Write down your list of options, prioritise the list, then tackle each task one by one.
- Think about what makes you happy. Write down a list of things you can focus on and goals that you can set that will help you develop personally and emotionally. Break those goals into small steps that you can act on each day. Schedule them into your day.
- Find time every single day to connect with your kids. If you feel like you don't have the patience to really be present, go back and focus on your personal goals.
- Reconnect with friends and family or find your single parent support tribe.

TOP TIPS

1. Be consistent.
2. Look for non-verbal cues. As I have learnt with Noah being non-verbal, you develop your own language without words. Even just by looking into his eyes you will know.
3. Figure out the motivation behind the tantrum.
4. Make time for fun.
5. Love hard. This one is easy. Just love. Show love. Give love. You won't regret it. Life is a funny thing, and no-one knows what could be around the corner, so live every day in love and love your people. I can't stress that enough.

MAUREEN O'SHAUGHNESSY

THE MINDSET OF AN ENTREPRENEUR

Many factors go into being a creative force for good – the best definition I have for an entrepreneur. Mindset is vital to our work as entrepreneurs. For me, it is a constant balancing act between striving, grounding and connecting. Curiosity, wellbeing, risk-taking and collaborating are the four aspects that drive my entrepreneurial efforts.

Being a curious, lifelong learner is the most important quality of an entrepreneur. I'm not just saying that because I'm coming from an educational perspective – honest! With this growth mindset, an entrepreneur values constantly learning in a wide variety of areas. Steven Kotler is one of my heroes. Founder of the Flow Research Collective, he is a neuroscientist who studies optimal flow and performance. Anyhow, Kotler practices what he preaches. He devours books on a variety of subjects. As he explains, our brain loves to constantly make connections. This ongoing learning gives our brain a plethora of ideas to play with and connect in new ways.

So, what are three ways I stoke curiosity and devour new information? I begin by asking LOTS of questions. Annoying as a two-year-old constantly asking *why,* I pepper others with questions. When I hear their genesis stories and understand the *why* behind their endeavors, I'm inspired. I also gain new resources or ideas from their *how.* These ideas can often be juxtaposed to my own efforts, helping me level up and enhance the services I offer. Connecting with others is so powerful – and I love sharing ideas and resources that I have, to spark ideas in others.

As an avid reader, I have audiobooks, ebooks and paper books all around me. This makes waiting in lines or on hold on the phone a breeze. I count this as 'found time' and use it to get in more reading. A cheat for audio books (and podcasts) is adjusting the speed. Sometimes I zip ahead at a 1.5x speed; other times I slow down or repeat a section to truly grasp a new concept.

Finally, podcasts are a gift to the lifelong learner! These snippets of information can help me deep dive into a topic or person. I can listen to the same person being interviewed by multiple podcasts and garner a fuller picture of the person of interest. Or I can 'graze' on a variety of fun topics offered by one podcast host or dabble with a variety of podcasts. There are so many great folks and ideas out there! True entrepreneurship is all about connecting variables in a new way to create a new resource.

Second to learning, we must make our wellbeing a priority. Many of us entrepreneurs have our switches stuck in the *on* position. We are so busy 'doing' that we forget to take care of our being. We must pay attention to the four pillars of health: nutrition, hydration, exercise and rest. Balancing the four and intentionally building them into our daily schedule keeps us able to bring on our A game.

Bringing the curiosity of a lifelong learner to our own fitness is very helpful. Wanting to understand the quality of my sleep, I started to track my heart rate variability and resting body temperature. I wanted to understand how my body is doing and what my heart rate looks like while I sleep. I didn't want emails coming through my wrist and other distracting data. So I researched and then invested in an Oura Ring that just gives me the body basics ... in an app. This focused information is used by many top athletes, and I value the insights I get. When I feel sluggish some mornings, I check the data and let the feedback guide the pace of my day.

I've also explored infrared saunas and begun to add this activity to my routine three to four times a week (as a cheat, I get great reading done in the sauna!). The advertised benefits of using infrared saunas include muscle and organ relaxation, detoxification, pain relief, improved cell health, better circulation, anti-aging, skin purification and weight loss. For me, the warmth (without feeling steamy suffocation!) is relaxing. It's a great way for me to begin to wind down and unplug before sleeping. As we take care of our health, we need to intentionally push our switches to the *off* position. Active recovery, out in nature, playing with children and pets, painting or moving – all rejuvenates us. AND I try to avoid screens, which do NOT help my brain get the recovery it needs. We all need to be at our physical best to serve others fully and create the cool changes we want for the world. Self-care is a necessity – never apologise for making your wellbeing a priority!

The third aspect for an entrepreneurial mindset is risk-taking. My daughter's best friend gave me a gift. It is a pink dish towel; on it is a picture of a girl wrestling an alligator. The quote says, 'Do one thing every day that scares your family!' I love the thought of being that alligator wrestler and not sliding into status quo or routine. Because I love to study 'flow' (that optimal mental state where time slides away and we are super-focused), I know that risk is a flow trigger and upsurges the amount of norepinephrine and dopamine in our systems.

Our brains don't know the difference between physical and non-physical risk. *Whew!* I can put myself into riskier social environments, creative environments or intellectual environments to trigger flow. No need to bungee jump to tap into the great benefits of added risk in my life. Public speaking (or even speaking up in a business meeting) can be that social risk we need to grow. Setting public goals or deadlines others are relying on can also add a sensation of risk.

One way to take risks is to try something new. Getting to be a beginner at something, especially with physical risk, charges our brains with cool chemicals. To explore this flow trigger and challenge myself, I have taken on aerial arts in the last few years. Being upside down and off the ground is definitely my alligator! The physical risk and skill required definitely keeps my 'head in the game' flowing, learning, and growing!

The final aspect in an entrepreneur's mindset is being able to be a polarity thinker. Right now, our world is becoming more binary and locked into *either/or* thinking. Based on a career of research and hard work, Barry Johnson of Polarity Partnerships has unpacked strategies to build on the best of both sides of a dilemma. In today's world of increasing interdependency and complexity, it is vital to utilise problem-solving with *both/and* thinking to address our most strategic challenges and opportunities.

I find this approach and these tools help me build bridges instead of divisions. Like appreciative inquiry, it lets me focus on the positive on both sides of a dynamic tension. And it keeps me from sliding into quick problem-solving fixes. When I work with students, we often play *'yes, and'* to build on other ideas and reframe our feedback. All measures that keep us working in a proactive and systemic manner, instead of a reactive one, are needed to grow the best solutions. *Ahh,* collaborating for win/win situations is a BIG gold standard of mine.

When we are curious, address our wellbeing, take challenges and embrace *both/and* thinking, we are at our best as entrepreneurs. From here, we can be a force for good and create solutions to make the world more equitable and humane. Works for me!

PERSONAL DEVELOPMENT JOURNEY

Just like happiness is an inside job, so is personal development. For me, personal and spiritual growth are interwoven. Spirituality, for me, is a broad sense that all is interconnected and love brings out the best in us. I don't need a certain creed, just to be fuelled by good and seeking closer alignment with my gifts and calling to serve. This journey is one of regular practices of reflection and connecting to what gives me joy.

I became aware that I was on this personal/spiritual journey when I was graduating from college. I had been a student board member for our college faith community. Because we were responsible for different parts of this ministry, the director had us check-in with her monthly. She wanted to make sure we were doing fine and using our gifts to take care of others and ourselves. As I was graduating, I realised I was going to miss this regular check-in and reflection time terribly. I told her how sad I was to have this end. She explained the process we had been using was called 'spiritual direction' and that I could find spiritual directors out in the 'real world'. *Hmmm, spiritual direction?* As I dove in, I discovered spiritual direction is similar to counselling. There is a person walking my personal growth journey with me – my spiritual director. Unlike counselling, there are no goals, especially not one of 'fixing' anything. The focus is on what brings me life and how I can shine out to others. Finding my first spiritual director and intentionally beginning this process as a young adult was empowering. I was hooked. Journalling, reading novels and poetry that made my heart sing and slowing down are key aspects I remember.

Along the way I became involved in the Ignatian Spiritual Exercises in Everyday Life (SEEL). The spiritual exercises are an unfolding series of prayers, meditations and reflections put together by Saint Ignatius of Loyola out of his own personal spiritual experience and those of others to whom he listened. This nine-month guided retreat focused on deep reflection and our growth edges. In the Catholic world, the Jesuits are educated and social justice oriented. Saint Ignatius had been their founder. So I was on this journey with a group of folks who were very dedicated to lifelong personal development and making a difference. It was humbling and empowering. After a year as a retreatant, I continued and was able to be a spiritual director for others making the retreat.

Retreats continued to be a time to step out of my daily life. I have taken various retreats over the years, including a week in an ashram in the Black Forest in Germany. My favourite were the silent retreats I took before the birth of each of my daughters. I went to a retreat centre (one time staying in a yurt) and let this be a time just for the baby about to be born. Writing them love songs, painting, taking long walks and telling the heartbeat within me my hopes and dreams for their happiness and wellbeing – this gift of time-out-of-time was priceless.

When I moved to the other side of the state to become a principal, I found a new spiritual director. Finding time for journalling and reflection was a big part of my process and a wonderful counter to the demands of running a school. Decades later I still meet with a spiritual director monthly.

Beyond regular reflection and walking my journey with a spiritual director, I have practices that help me rebalance. Like many entrepreneurs, I am a driver. I make lists and get stuff done! Sometimes I don't stop until I am exhausted. This is not ideal. In my doctoral program I took an elective that tied into our spiritual journeys. I wrote a paper on time from the Greek god lens of Kronos and Kairos. Kronos represents measured time. It is very regimented and linear – just like I am when I am trying to accomplish a task. While Kronos and structure helps me open a school, write a book or start a podcast, it lacks soul for me. Kairos, on the other hand, is a timeless flow. This ancient Greek word means the perfect moment or timing, the opportune moment, the moment of truth, the defining moment, that fleeting moment that comes and goes in the blink of an eye, which must be seized and not let go. Kairos is quality, not quantity. For me, this is when I step back and am not task driven. Maybe it's when I get a call, 'Mom, can we talk right now?' or embrace a yearning to take a walk in the woods. I try hard to remember to balance Kronos and Kairos. This frame for how we view time has stayed a powerful reminder for me over the years. I find it easy to get locked into chronological tasks and appointments. But Kairos time-out-of-time is when I reground myself and I'm happiest.

The best book I've found for guidance on creative time that recharges my spirit is *The Artist's Way*. Author Julia Cameron helps people with artistic creative recovery, and teaches techniques and exercises to assist people in harnessing their creative talents and skills. Often this book is the subject of a book study group or weekly art session. Cameron shares many strategies for an authentic personal development journey. A favourite of mine, that enhances my spiritual journey, is the Artist's Date. The Artist's Date is a weekly gift where we are encouraged to explore something creative. Whether it's going to a museum, blowing glass figurines in a studio, watching interpretive dance at your local college or exploring a new neighborhood – building a regular commitment to exploration and creativity enlightens us.

Entrepreneurs – we are wired to build and make things happen. Don't let it come at the cost of not also building time for ourselves. Kronos needs to be balanced with Kairos. Exploration and creating just for joy are necessities. Making our personal development journey a priority is incredibly important to staying grounded as we use our gifts fully to make the world a better place. It is not selfish. It is putting on our own oxygen mask first – so that we have maximum energy and momentum to be a force for good. Find your spiritual muses/directors and invest in your Kairos time-out-of-time. It will truly enhance your leadership.

Those who love you or look up to you will appreciate your example of self-care and the good energy you bring to everything around you.

BUSINESS ADVICE

Shakespeare's, 'To thine own self be true,' is excellent business advice. Before we can dive into a business idea or prospect, we need to be grounded in who we are and what we are called to do. Then we can take stock of where we are and where we want to go. And finally, we can pivot within that knowledge as life evolves. Let's start with becoming grounded in our reason for being and using it to create our North Star.

The Japanese have a philosophy of *ikigai*. This is their reason for being – for jumping out of bed in the morning. Fuelled by purpose, the people on the Japanese island of Okinawa live longer than folks anywhere else in the world. Their model is simple and profound – wonderful advice for any business. They look at four components and place them in separate circles on a Venn diagram. Where these circles overlap is their ikigai; they pursue that common factor with great energy.

Ask yourself these four questions to determine the labels of your four components:

1. What am I good at?
2. What do I love?
3. What does the world need?
4. What can I be paid for?

Let's unpack each.

- What I am good at. Most of us have a pretty good sense of what we are *not* good at. I can problem solve and motivate others, but you would not want me designing anything mechanical or driving large vehicles! We are drawn to experiences that feel good, which usually correlate to having skill at or fun with the endeavor. Think about roles you played informally, perhaps in a social group or on a team. Are you the organiser? The enthusiast? The dogged get-it-done person? The thoughtful person tuning in on details? What do others say you are good at? Ask five of your friends to list your talents and strengths. Maybe you haven't given yourself enough credit for some of your talents! Circle your top three strengths.

- What I love. What fills you with joy? For one of my daughters, animals and caring for others lights her up. For the other, leading and activism. For me? Creating, connecting and youth. Think of hobbies you enjoy. Where are you in your zone? We have passions for a reason. We all do better when we are fuelled by joy. List what lights you up. Circle your top three joys.

- What the world needs. I've heard this question expressed as, 'What breaks your heart?' Do you feel sad seeing stray dogs? Upset when you think of the refugee or homeless crisis? Lament the plummeting mental health of our youth? Get frustrated when looking at litter and plastic bottles everywhere? Maybe you are an environmentalist or humanitarian. List the top three world problems that evoke strong feelings.

- What I can be paid for. The first three categories can suffice if you are not trying to make a living. When I retire, I may volunteer in a humanitarian capacity. But for now, let's look at the intersection of the first three components.

These tell you what your purpose might be. Where might what I am good at, love and the world needs intersect in a way that gets paid for? Play with the possibilities for a bit. Seek out more information on businesses or products that line up with your other three ikigai components. Question what you might create that plays to your strengths, passions and a world need. List at least three possibilities. This may include a possible business you could start.

Putting the four components together lines you up with your unique reason for being. It takes self-awareness. Many will want to sell you an 'opportunity' that does not align with your ikigai. Be open, yet discerning.

Another way to get clear on what business might be worthy of your life energy is to write your mission statement. nXu Education guides youth and young adults in clarifying their ikigai and writing their life purpose statement. This mission statement becomes a North Star as you look at business possibilities. Begin with identity – who are you? A parent, an entrepreneur, a person of privilege? Then look at purpose by combining strengths and what is loved. Conclude with the change that you will make in the world. Try to make this life purpose statement under thirty-five words. Let me share what I came up with, doing this nXu exercise with my students:

As a privileged white mom and activist, I use my experience and passion for youth combined with my love of forging connections and overcoming obstacles to be a catalyst for transforming schools into places of love, belonging, passion and purpose, with thriving and future-ready teens.

Months later, this life purpose statement still resonates. You will know when you've pulled your ikigai into this North Star. You will feel the rightness of it.

Once you have your ikigai and North Star, you are ready to take inventory of where you are and where you want to go. Maybe you are fairly aligned with your values and only want to add a component. Maybe you are ready for a complete overhaul. Don't do this heavy lifting in isolation. Talk to lots of other people – those who know you professionally and personally, as well as those who are doing work that appeals to you. Generate lots of ideas and possibilities. Expect this to take time.

Know that you can constantly reinvent yourself. You never arrive. Maureen 1.0 has evolved through 2.0 and is heading to 3.0 ... it's a journey. Every time I move to a new location or have a life transition, I re-evaluate. What do I want more of? Less of? What is calling me? Where do I want to grow? This allows adjustments for a new child in my life, or a change in health or more leisure time.

I also spend time annually on two New Year's reflections, instead of writing resolutions. I schedule the directions for each on my calendar, on repeat. On 27 December, I follow the process used by my friend Jessica Butts. I reread my journals from the past year. In a new journal I note themes, learnings about myself, what worked, one to three key words I used. Then I write a letter to myself to read the next 27 December. I tell myself what I want more of so I can ROAR. And what I want to say *no* to.

On 29 December, I do the 'Past Year Review' suggested by Tim Ferriss. It takes less than an hour and is very informative. I note a *positive* and *negative* column on a piece of paper. Then I go through my calendar from the past year and look at each week. I note any people, activities or commitments that triggered peak positive or negative emotions in the respective column.

After I've gone through the year, I review the list and look for the 20% in each column that produced the most consistent or powerful peaks. For the positives, I get them on my calendar immediately. Book it on the calendar to make it real. Prior to the pandemic, this meant booking and then going out dancing the first week in January – scheduling-in joy felt great! The other task is to take the top negatives and create a *NOT-TO-DO LIST*. I post this in my office where I can see it each morning during January. As Tim says, 'These are the people and things you *know* make you miserable, so don't put them on your calendar out of obligation, guilt, FOMO or other nonsense.' Don't just take out the negative or the void fills quickly with low priorities. Proactively calendar-in your positives.

To thine own self be true. Self-knowledge is the most important business knowledge. When you bring this authentic, whole being to whatever business endeavor you pursue, you are destined to go far. Good luck!

OVERCOMING ADVERSITY

Sometimes situations really are horrible. There is no way to soften the blow. A friend is killed. I am fired from a job. My child makes a painful decision and I can't do anything to fix it. In these situations it isn't about overcoming anything. For me, it's about slowing my world down and making time for the emotions. I get to be human. When I try to push through it, I become brittle and disconnected. It's worth it to take the healing time. I let go of all non-essentials and get very gentle with myself. I listen to my body and soul, and respond accordingly. I cry, rant, take long walks and eat comfort food. I give myself this break. It's uncomfortable and I don't like it. But this is how I heal.

Time is my friend. Strong feelings fade. In one spiritual group, we did an activity that helped give me a new perspective on adversity. We were asked to list four devastating experiences from our past. And then we were asked to find the upside from each experience. My first devastation had been not getting to go away to the college where my parents and brother had gone. I got a generous scholarship to my hometown university and it made sense to stay local. To my eighteen-year-old mind it was such a let-down. But looking back, I am grateful that this cost savings allowed me to study in Mexico and Spain. Travelling and living in these countries launched me into a career in international schools. My eighteen-year-old self could never have seen a positive outcome, but it was there.

A later adversity was the miscarriage of my first pregnancy. This loss still tugs at my heartstrings. But I truly can't imagine not having the two amazing daughters I have. They are such a source of constant wonder and deep love. They wouldn't exist without that first miscarriage. On life's big losses, I learned to trust that time and perspective will soften them. I see a spiritual component that comforts me and helps me move on.

In terms of daily setbacks, I watch my students ride the roller-coaster of adolescent emotions. Happy times are responded to with exuberant joy. Obstacles or setbacks are responded to with desolation and defeat. I am so grateful to not be a tween or teen! The level of energy these responses take would exhaust me instantly. Being older, I have had more time on this roller-coaster of life with its many highs and lows. This longer perspective fills me with hope. I know that adversity is not permanent, so I don't get knocked off my feet with every obstacle. I also know that victories can be fleeting, so I soak them up with gratitude.

So how can we overcome adversity and not wallow in defeat? A big part of the equation is knowing myself and playing to my strengths. I will stretch, but I am not going to pursue areas that are completely outside my wheelhouse. I also know my temperament. I am not the person who can deal with daily procedures and details. I need to create, influence and be a force for change.

So one way I overcome adversity is by avoiding paths I should not be walking down.

In my doctoral program we looked at systems. This perspective of seeing the many layers and parts of an organisation is very helpful. In my work with schools, there are the family systems and dynamics that influence individual students. There is the school system and their expectations of what a graduate will look like. There are the teaching teams and how they interact with each other, the content and the students. There are the boards and how they oversee the governance. Each part of the system must work together like the gears of a machine. When I forget to look at both the whole machine and the individual gears, I lose my systemic perspective. And that's when adversity likes to strike.

But thinking systemically is not enough. I need to embrace the innate ebbs and flows of any situation. I worked with a spiritual director who used a lovely metaphor that helped me deal with adversity and setbacks. Using the metaphor of a garden, she reminded me that the work of caring for a garden is never done. That there are seasons that require weeding, fertilising or the earth lying fallow. In this mindfulness practice she appreciates all of the seasons. She sees their importance to the whole and doesn't just appreciate the spring and summer months when we enjoy the fruits of our labour. She expects to be doing cyclical work for the overall good of the garden. I admit this metaphor stretches me. I don't naturally appreciate the times of weeding or pruning in my business. And sometimes there seems to be more fertiliser in a situation than I would like!

My teen students get extremely caught up in the drama of adversity. They live so fully in the present moment that everything is of heightened importance. But with more life experience, I can see the patterns and value this systemic approach that makes adversity a smaller, more manageable part of the equation. Please take time to sense and respond to the big setbacks. And trust time will be your friend. There will be life after a setback. And possibly some new opportunities or insights as a silver lining to your adversity. As the saying goes, we just need to get up one more time than we are knocked down. You can do it!

GOALS AND GOAL SETTING

The ikigai and life purpose statement I unpacked in the business advice section guide my goals. From this foundation, it's really important to create and implement a system of setting and reviewing goals and progress made.

Getting focused can be challenging for me – I love the ideas and exploring possibilities. So John Doerr's book, *Measure What Matters: How Google, Bono, and the Gates Foundation Rock the World with OKRs* was a priceless find. John says, 'Ideas are easy. Execution is everything.' And, 'We must realise – and act on the realisation – that if we try to focus on everything, we focus on nothing.' Luckily, he then breaks it down into a system, 'An effective goal-setting system starts with disciplined thinking at the top, with leaders who invest the time and energy to choose what counts.' This system is called OKRs and stands for *objectives* and *key results*. These are similar to the SMART goals I was familiar with. But OKRs stretch me to accomplish more.

The first part of an OKR is the *objective:* this is WHAT will be achieved. It's as simple as that. The second part of an OKR are the *key results:* the HOW you will accomplish your objective. Key results are measurable. Accomplishing all key results should equate to accomplishing your objective. OKRs help me identify my priorities and place my focus there. All tasks are not of equal importance!

My friend, Danny Bauers (Better Leaders Better Schools),

quantifies the OKRs with a point system for partial or full completion of each key result. If you are a numbers person, this gives you regular data. I'm not a big numbers person. So, I just set the goal of completing a certain number (usually three) daily goals leading to the objectives. This can be gamified, but that doesn't work for me. I set my phone alarm to play a happy-dance-end-of-work-day song and aspire to have the goals met by then. I also need to sprinkle lots of inspirational quotes and affirmations into my goal list to fire me up – and keep the numbers from overloading my brain.

Let me break down my system.

From my life purpose statement comes a big audacious goal. I call it my massively transformative purpose (MTP). It has the dreaded numbers in it to make it measurable:

I am a world influence for revolutionising equitable/inclusive secondary education. This results in the creation of 101 learner-centered/agency-driven learning communities where students thrive, follow passion and purpose, and become future-ready contributors to do good in the world.

Then I created a spreadsheet. I begin by listing ten 'high hard goals' to achieve my MTP. This list goes from one to ten years out. I'm pleased that I've reached two of these goals this year:

- By June 2022: To give my TEDx Talk on Action Toward New High School Paradigm.
- By July 2021: To have launched EdActive Collective and Summit.

1. Early in my career, Stephen Covey was an inspiration. His framework of looking at my various roles and setting goals for each has stuck with me. So, I create annual goals for my roles of being a podcaster, consultant, happy and healthy being, school leader, mastermind leader, etc.

2. Then, on the same MTP spreadsheet, I break the goals into smaller parts of:

- Quarterly.
- Monthly.
- Weekly.

3. Finally, I calendar-in quarterly days, monthly mornings and Friday blocks to review the MTP and analyse my progress. This time is sacred to me. I work hard to not let other 'urgent' tasks take me away from this 'important' (Covey's quadrants) work.

I'm a super random person. Routines feel very heavy and burdensome. My playful inner child balks at activities that feel constricting. If you also have this temperament, here are six strategies that might make your goal setting practice more playful and appealing.

1. Use colour! I love the spark of energy colour gives me. So I change up fonts and colours when I work, especially in my weekly MTP sheet. I also use different markers and types of papers when I'm jotting notes or handwriting lists. It keeps my brain finding the variety it needs to stay engaged.

2. Use affirmations or mantras. I am a big believer in *I statements* in the present tense. Very woo-woo, I know. I get daily happy quotes from Tut.com in my inbox to remind me of the magical, wonderful nature of existence. And I use affirmations – sometimes written out repeatedly, to own the next steps in my journey or overcome a limiting belief. *I create spaciousness and my day flows with a balance of work and play,* would be a great affirmation for me today!

3. Add music and/or movement. Music taps into different parts of our brains. It can energise and focus us. I tend to get distracted, so it keeps my brain happy while I'm working on a task. I use a playlist of instrumental music played very softly when I'm writing a blog or deep in planning. I use a 'fired-up' playlist to run sprints or turbo through house cleaning. And I use *Mambo #5* to gear up for a podcast interview and as my daily 5pm end-of-day dance celebration.

4. Celebrate with fun rituals. Whether it is a cup of coffee after morning stretches, starting meetings with a quirky connection question, or a year-end goofy award ceremony with your work team – rituals enhance our processes. I use them to add joy to my day.

5. Buddy up. Cicero nailed it: 'Friendship improves happiness and abates misery, by the doubling of our joy and the dividing of our grief.' Accountability buddies, mastermind groups, personal fitness trainers, spiritual directors – there are so many ways to make sure you have the support you deserve. Claim it!

6. Mix it up. When I was a little girl, sometimes we would have pancakes for dinner. The silliness of breakfast for dinner delighted me. Then as a kindergarten teacher (the one year I was crazy enough to teach the wee ones!), I would run our day in reverse before having a substitute teacher. These delightful children could get so locked into 'that's not how our teacher does it' that I used this practice to remind the class that there are many ways things can be done and that variety is fun. The substitute teacher appreciated my help getting kids out of fixed thinking! Nowadays, when I have a non-preferred task to complete, I look for ways to mix it up, possibly adding silliness. Maybe I'm in a serious

Zoom meeting wearing footy pajamas on the part of me not on the screen. Or flossing (that wonky kid dance) on a walk in the neighbourhood to appall my adult daughter walking with me. Mixing things up definitely gives my brain the novelty and fun it so loves!

So, align your goals to your North Star, break them down, create a system to measure and review them, and get started! The world needs your genius!

TOP TIPS

- Trust it's mind over matter. Our thoughts create our reality. Claim your purpose and superpowers. Affirm your goals in present tense. (i.e. *I am a world-class educational consultant, influencing inclusive, engaging and equitable learning on a global scale.*) Know it. Own it. Be it.

- Be laser-like focused. You have only an on-off switch. Either an idea or project helps you level up or it doesn't. Rabbit holes and detours abound. Protect your resources of time and energy. Know what is yours to do and do it.

- Set daily goals. The night before, set the next day's three to five goals and get everything ready to dive in first thing in the morning.

- Create and stick with systems. Automate as much of your life as possible. Chunk like tasks into common groups of time. Turn off notifications. Limit email responses to once or twice daily.

- Love yourself. When you've met your daily goals, turn your switch off. Exercise. Play. Share time with loved ones. Recharge your batteries. You are more than enough. You are a unique and wonderful gift to humanity. Own it and take care of your precious self.

SARAH
BLAKE

THE MINDSET OF AN ENTREPRENEUR

The transition from being in business to becoming an entrepreneur is all about the mindset shift. For me, I had always had a dream of running my own business and of serving the community. For eight years I successfully ran a small home-based business that brought in income and enabled me the flexibility to care for our two young children whilst my husband served in the forces. It was working – I was busy, and my reputation meant that I didn't have to market beyond networking. But this wasn't enough. I realised that my passive approach to my business, as distinct from my profession, was actually limiting my growth. Worse, it was limiting me and my ability to make a difference.

I realised that something needed to change, that what I was doing was actually unsustainable. I was stuck in a reactive rhythm of create leads, work, pause for school holidays and start the cycle again. My mindset needed to shift.

I needed to take a long, hard and painful look at *me*. What I saw was someone working harder and harder but with little capacity for growth, and it was compromising the very things that I wanted to achieve – flexibility for my family, financial freedom and the capacity to help people turn conflict into opportunity. The hard reality was that I had reached a plateau. Rather than let this disappointment ruin me, I became excited about change. I was ready to do things differently and so began my transformation.

This shift in momentum doesn't just happen. It is an evolution and I had started the journey, taken my first steps towards an unapologetically big dream.

Like any journey, growth is a process. We can short circuit the hard work for instant gratification, or we can lean into the hard work of getting the foundations right. For many of us that means going back to basics and clearing the ground of the debris that may have held us back. This entrepreneurial spirit is, to some extent, an essence of courage. You need to be brave to look inside and you need to be brave to step beyond the safe boxes that people like to put around you.

For me, the process of levelling up began with the recognition that I couldn't do this by myself. What had served me in the past would no longer serve my growth into the future. But the first port of call was me – I needed to find what mattered to this new me, what was it that I really wanted to achieve, what was the thing I could best contribute to the world?

So here are my mindset lessons that are carrying me into the future.

MINDSET LESSON ONE – SELF-BELIEF

I'm not talking about the shallow, ego-driven desire to be famous or the self-entitled belief that you are amazing. An entrepreneurial mindset requires you to really believe in what you are working towards. It requires you to find that deep, gritty strength within yourself. That you matter and that what you have to offer the world matters. *Why?* – because this is hard work – you will face the setbacks, failure and disappointment; you will have to work harder than you have before and it is this self-belief that helps to push you forward – it is your beacon of hope.

For me, helping people respond to conflict is a vocation. I have carried this drive for as long as I can remember. I may not be the best, I may not have all the knowledge, but I know that what I do have is important. That I have a responsibility to share and help others because of the gifts that I have been given. I recognised that in diminishing my light, my limited beliefs were undermining my vocation. This realisation created a rapid shift in mindset – I gave myself permission to dream BIG.

MINDSET LESSON TWO – CLARITY OF PURPOSE

So, you've given yourself permission to dream, you are excited about the potential and you know in your bones that this shift is for you. This shift is about investing in your business, not just your profession – this is the thing that distinguishes you from the rest. But it can also be a trap if not treated with respect.

Creating clarity of purpose has really elevated my growth – we hear the word *niche* so much but why does that matter? When we create that clear vision we are able to block out all the extra noise. We are better able to hold the boundaries and not get swept up in trends and shiny distractions. It creates a consistency of thought, action and outcome. So, as you foster this new mindset shift, take the time to discover your vision. Write it down, revisit it, sharpen and hone it.

For me, in naming that vision, of being brave enough to dream big, I was able to release it to the world. I became unapologetically proud of what I wanted to achieve and I was ready to really own it. Having clarity about this purpose helps you to stay connected to your heart not just your ego. It is your check-in point that both holds you to account and inspires you to keep stepping forward.

MINDSET LESSON THREE – CLEAR THE BLOCKAGES

We all have battle wounds, unconscious scars that shape who we are and what we do. As an entrepreneur, you can't ignore these fracture points as you could have before. This is the long game we are playing, and eventually these blockages will impact your movement. So, we need to be brave enough to do the internal work, because your integrity and authenticity are reflected in the quality of the outcomes you achieve.

I grew up with a father who dreamed big but struggled with the realities, and a mother who solidly delivered but was afraid to dream big. On the most part, the messages I heard about money were that 'making money was bad' – it meant you were selfish and greedy and didn't care for community. To make money meant that somehow you had compromised your ethics and values by placing money over people. It is hard to acknowledge that I had let this 'false' story limit my relationship with money and growth. Again, I needed to heal that wound, so that my mindset evolution could continue.

I did the work; I still do the work. In naming that weakness I have created the strategies that help me move forward. I sought inspiration from the people who have demonstrated that you can make money and value people. That heart-centred entrepreneurial growth is possible and exciting, and that the financial benefits will only enhance my capacity to make a difference and give back. Interestingly, it has also meant that I now value myself as I should have – I understand my own worth.

MINDSET LESSON FOUR – DISCIPLINE

Nothing easy creates lasting outcomes. Becoming an entrepreneur isn't something that you wake up one day and decide that is what you are. You have to be willing to invest in the craft, hone your professional skills and be learning all the time. It takes real discipline and you have to be prepared to get down and work, get your hands dirty in the mess and reality of life.

It takes discipline to resist the temptations of quick fixes and shallow action. It takes discipline to focus your time and outputs, and it is disciplined practise that ensures you analyse, ask questions and align action with purpose.

I am not naturally a structured person; I am creative, I am

super comfortable with uncertainty and flexibility and trust the universe. But it is also critical that I bring discipline to what I do and how I do it.

An entrepreneurial mindset is able to hold the line and remain focused. That discipline applies to ourselves, our business and how we influence the world. The truly successful entrepreneur is one who has created the systems that enable these elements to shine consistently forward.

Levelling up isn't really about your product, that is just the means to the end. What matters, in essence what your super-power emerges from, is your mindset. Taking that first step is sometimes the hardest shift, but your courage and willingness to be vulnerable is you taking responsibility for your future, the future of your family and perhaps even the future of our world.

JUDE
MORROW

When Icarus took to the skies in the ancient Greek tale, he was brimming with confidence. He flew higher and higher. Soared into the sky, despite being told to not fly too high, or indeed, fly too low. In today's world, mindset and believing everything is possible has taken the world by storm. What I ask of you is, is there such thing as flying too high? Is there a level of success that makes you forget yourself?

OVERCOMING ADVERSITY

For as long as I could remember, I was always different. I interact with the world differently; I see perspectives others do not and a lot of my comfort zones can be greatly challenged at times. I was always the outsider, the external observer, and the one who always spent his time wondering how he could be like everyone else. It is very difficult to explain exactly what it's like to be different. The reason why I am different, is because I am autistic.

Throughout my early life, everybody wanted to support me. I knew that everybody had their hearts in the right place for me, and that everybody wanted me to succeed. The sad thing is, when you are autistic – or different in any way – the onus is always on *you* to change, not everyone else. I can fully recognise that so many went out of their way to help me, and for this I am grateful, but I couldn't help but feel like a broken version of everybody else.

Growing up in the school system, I was always the one that was eager to be noticed, and I developed a persona that was clearly not my own, to fit in with everyone else and feel like I was part of the group. This is a phenomenon called 'masking'. Masking is not something that is specifically related to the autistic community – it is experienced by a vast majority of people at certain points in their life.

I didn't really socialise much, and although I gave off a confident and assured personality, inside I was full of bitter hatred for the fact that I wasn't like everyone else around me. Not everyone in the world is autistic, the generally accepted figure as approximately 1.5 to 2.5% of the world's population. As an adult I developed a toxic goal, my goal was to prove my doubters wrong, or at least the doubters I believed that I had.

When I came to my late teens, I was still at school, and I needed to find a career that would be most suited to me. I had started to attend a local cross-community group, as autism groups like those that exist now weren't really around when I was a late teenager in the late 2000s. Although, at this group, I had a particular strength that was put to very good use.

I found myself enjoying completing funding application forms, and tenaciously chasing replies. I also found myself being the person that people would come to ask advice from. Given that some 'accepted social nuances' can pass me by, I would be one that would be brutally honest. This made me realise that I was quite proficient in problem-solving, and I got a sense of satisfaction knowing that I was able to look at a situation logically and give the best advice for people even if it was hard for them to hear at times.

I even felt good about myself that I was a decent problem solver! The medical textbooks would say that autistic people can have *social difficulties* and *do not understand the feelings of others*. I wanted to blow that stereotype out of the water with my career choice. The world would have you believe that autistic people either work in menial jobs for virtue signalling 'autism work initiatives', or work in the most scientific or mathematical of environments. Not me! I decided to become a social worker and that was a career I held onto for eight years!

My experience covered many different fields: care of the

elderly and intellectually disabled, and in both the statutory and voluntary sectors. For the most part, it was a career that I reasonably enjoyed, at least when both my head and heart were in the game. I had applied my strengths wherever I could, I found myself good at completing funding applications, giving sound advice and being able to visualise positive strategies and positive outcomes for others.

PERSONAL DEVELOPMENT JOURNEY

By the time I was twenty-two, I thought that I had conquered the world. To me, autism was something that I had beaten. It was a part of my past that would not define my future. Given the negative press and a lot of negativities propelled by medical businesses and charities, it made me believe as an adult, being autistic was only for little kids, and indeed, something to feel ashamed about. The thought that in the years to follow, I would be not only proud, but publicly open about being autistic, would have been met with my trademark sprinkle of cynicism.

As a twenty-two-year-old, I had gathered plenty of early wins and successes for someone my age. I managed to buy a car, I graduated from university and went into a very well-paid social work job and had a plan in place for the rest of my life.

In late 2012, my life changed. I learned that I was going to become a dad! This caused me to have a whole wave of emotions. First, I would love to say excitement was the dominant emotion, but it wasn't. Fear won that race every day of the week, including Sunday! Don't forget, only a short number of years prior, I had a classroom assistant and had to rely on additional educational supports to get through my day. How would I cope raising a little child? The fact I didn't accept that I was autistic earlier in life, bred a toxic thought process in my mind. I was more focused on how I could make myself look successful, and without internal struggle.

When my son was born on 23 July 2013, he slotted into my routine very nicely at first. I suppose I fit the stereotype quite well, in that I do have a particular thirst and longing for routine and can be averse to change. Although, as biology dictates, my little boy started to grow. He started to walk, talk and like different things. I was always taking this personally. A lot of my interests I have had from my earliest days and they remain with me now. In my own mind, structure and rigidity are what keeps society and architecture grounded.

I wanted to be like Icarus. I wanted to make the shiniest wings, made of the most exquisite waxes and feathers, and fly as high as I could. I wanted to prove to my son that I wasn't a failure, or a broken person. I had so many feelings of self-inadequacy that it made me do everything I could to hide them from my son's view.

Many in the world of mindset are familiar with the term 'burning desire'. I had this too, in abundance! Although my burning desire was to show the world I was a success and had overcome so much, perhaps so much so that I was not always present with those around me, especially my family. I have no doubt that burning desire is good – burning desire can serve you incredibly well, however when the burning desire burns those around you, it is time to rethink things.

I came home from work one evening in September 2015. At the time, I worked in a busy community mental health team thirty miles from home, and the dreary drive was a tough part of my daily routine. I came home and my mother had told me that Ethan had asked her a question.

'Why does Daddy always look so sad?'

My struggle for self-acceptance was so clear that even my three-year-old son could see it. This is when I knew I had to change. I had to finally learn to accept myself for who I was. I had to undergo months of counselling and cognitive behaviour therapy (CBT), to reframe my thinking. I realised that my life was not one challenge after another, but more like one victory after another. I suddenly started to become proud of all that I had achieved to that point in my life, and it felt wonderful.

There is still terrible stigma in seeking mental health care today, one that I work every day to try and remove. If your mind goes to darker places, do not ignore it. The answers and solutions you need should never be hidden by any forms of false positivity, in the same way a rattle within a car's engine can never be 'fixed' by turning your car radio to a higher volume. Professional help and support is absolutely nothing to be ashamed of – you are not weak, you are not inadequate, and seeking help and guidance is one of the biggest shows of strength you could possibly do.

GOALS & GOAL SETTING

After coming to a state of self-acceptance, I wanted to share my story. I didn't want other people to feel the same way I did, and to give parents hope that autistic children, like me, even though I am now in my thirties and have a beard, can grow up to live happy and successful lives. When undergoing CBT, I kept all my notebooks from each session, to revisit certain points of my childhood, teenage years and early adulthood. I have always been a prolific writer, although just for myself. I wouldn't call myself a 'diarist' as such, not in the same fashion as Adrian Mole, Anne Frank or 'Wimpy Kid', but I thought that I would write down my thoughts, and as the pen slides along the pages, the vision appears and then I act upon it.

I would encourage everyone to do this. If you have an idea, write it down! The idea you write down may become the idea that propels your journey to success and abundance. When I laid out all my notebooks, I decided that I wanted to compile them into a memoir, and I did! I had a goal to tell my story, not for the masses, but for my son. I wanted him to know what my journey was like and try to turn it into something positive and insightful that people can learn from.

When I realised that my own story resonated with so many people, I decided to try and single-handedly change the world forever for autistic people like me. I had always had a taste for lofty goals, and whether or not I believed in myself fully through-out my life, I was always a dreamer. I decided that I would put these dreams to good use, rather than my own personal use of proving everybody wrong at every turn.

I love visual learning. I love writing things down and then seeing the road ahead become more and more clear. Almost like directing a huge spotlight in front of me and seeing the trees, plants, grass, puppies, rainbows and sunshine ahead! Although with the most wonderful thing in the world – hindsight – I wish I had uncovered some of the things I will pass on to you in this chapter.

With a debut book that did well, came plenty of opportuni-ties. I didn't go in search of the limelight, but somehow, I found myself in it, and for the most part I enjoyed it! I got to meet more autistic people like me and decided to devote my life, career and ambitions to Neurodiversity Training International – the vehi-cle to which global perceptions about autism and autistic people would change.

I had it all mapped out in one of my trusted notepads! I would deliver training and consultancy on a global scale and change the narrative from 'disordered' to 'gifted' and find myself on the most prestigious speaking stages in the world. For the most part, this happened! I was blessed to deliver keynote speeches on global stages, grace the TEDx stage twice and have a solid list of media appearances.

After I came into the public consciousness, I had all the right ideas. I wanted to create a global utopia where autistic people like me could flourish, and celebrate their differences, rather than constantly feeling that we need to be fixed or repaired to fit into a society not made for us. By this stage, I had crafted the perfect set of wings and was soaring higher than I ever dreamt that I could. Sadly, I realised that for every set of wings there are out there, there stands someone with a pair of giant scissors, ready to seize their opportunity to cut them from you. I have confessed to be many things before – being vain, consumed with a desire to be noticed both by my peers and the public, being extremely flattered by praise and feeling dismayed when my accomplishments aren't recognised publicly.

One thing I am immensely proud of is that I have never found myself keen to sabotage the success of other people. When you are entering business regarding a particular social cause, it is normal to think that you will 'find your tribe', that the tribe will immediately take you in and listen to your voice. In a lot of cases, that is true – you will find your tribe and luckily, I have found mine, although the analogy of kissing frogs comes to mind.

My first nugget of gold for you: never ever expect everyone to view you with adulation. I naively thought that this would happen. There are so many people out there that had the same message as me, and likely that will be out there for you, too! No matter what field you work in or operate your business from, there will always be collaborators, competitors and haters. Deep down, I knew the latter two existed, but refused to plan or prepare for them in any way whatsoever. This was a fatal flaw.

I have always been someone who has felt criticism and ridicule much more acutely than the average person, but when I started growing and scaling my own business, more and more haters came out of the woodwork and descended. I refused to believe that this would happen to me, and as you grow, this will certainly happen to you. With visibility comes both growth, and if you are visible to more people, the chances of some of those people feeling threatened by you become much higher.

It doesn't matter what niche you are in, there will be a 'top table' of influencers who you will want to get close to. Like the famous marketing exercise of having a 'Dream 100' people to help you grow your business, add value to and all the rest. I am not criticising the Dream 100 method as it helped me immensely – all you need to do is collate a list of twenty-five people in these four categories: bloggers, podcasters, influencers and business owners. I did this as a labour of love and for the most part, it worked! I was able to collaborate and add value to many people, and in turn, this added immense value for me too.

Sadly, there were a couple on there who didn't see me as anything other than a threat. I was a threat to their imaginary top table of neurodiversity advocacy and consultancy. This was a very bitter pill to swallow for me, as I would never feel threatened by another person. I only see opportunities, not threats. Nobody ever knows how far they will soar, unpredictability and luck exist for a reason, but everybody knows one thing, the people that stood with scissors.

If you ever feel threatened by someone else's success in life, that obviously suggests an inner turmoil that may only be corrected by professional help. How successful people become, and remain, successful is by seeing opportunities in places, people and things. When it comes to people, we are the evillest species in the animal kingdom, and we do not do ourselves any favours by tearing down others. Even if a new kid arrives on the block – one with a stronger message or better branding – support their journey even if it means they surpass you in the invisible hierarchy. The reason I say this is because there could be an abundance of value that they can give to you down the road.

I have never forgotten those who helped and supported me to build a thriving seven-figure training and consultancy business in a matter of months. I now look for infinite ways to serve them, add value to them and collaborate with them. What I never forget are those who were waiting on the sidelines with a shiny pair of scissors to cut me down at every opportunity. Whilst not outwardly, my internal response to them involves a double-digited hand gesture, an expletive, followed by the word *off*. Blowing out someone else's candle doesn't make yours burn brighter.

THE MINDSET OF AN ENTREPRENEUR

Given that I am an avid learner, I always want to learn things. One of the gifts of being autistic is that when I take interest in something, I must know everything about it. I watched AMC's series *The Terror,* which gave a historical fiction account of Sir John Franklin's doomed sea expedition to the Canadian Arctic to chart the Northwest Passage in 1845, to find a shortcut from Europe to Asia.

The two ships HMS Erebus and HMS Terror became stuck in the pack ice in late 1845, they were stuck for three years, and the crew's beloved Captain Sir John Franklin died on 11 June 1847 before the ships were deserted by their crews in April 1848. The crew intended to march south through King William Island to reach the Back Fish River – and civilisation – but all died out in the arctic void.

After watching this, I read every single Google page about the historical expedition, watched every documentary I could and it became what an observer would call, an 'obsession'. I even know that the expedition brought with them; 32,000lbs of tinned food, 200gal of wine for the sick, 9,300lbs of lemon juice to fight off scurvy, one hundred Bibles, 1,000lbs of mustard, 7,000lbs of tobacco, a room full of muskets/rifles and one daguerreotype camera.

I turned this thirst for knowledge into my business. I wanted to learn absolutely everything there is to know about growing and scaling my training and consultancy business. All the books, you name them, I read them! All the social media groups, I joined them and even listened to every podcast that I could. When you start a business or a movement, you will come across challenges, and I certainly did. I remember reading in the past that a large percentage of the most successful people ever to have lived, were autistic. Surely there was one single trait they all had that pro-pelled them into cultural greatness. That gift was problem-solving.

Using this logic, I thought that the onus was on me to learn everything I could to improve any tough situations I was in. The main challenge I had at first was building a snazzy website and developing my web presence. I immediately found myself search-ing the internet for every single *how-to* guide and reading every *Five steps/how to build a brilliant website* article. As hours and days disappeared, I found myself being no further forward. I was never gifted in the field of technology or the internet. If I could get away with it, I would still write with a feather and ink, and calculate everything using an abacus. I am an old soul at heart, one thing I realised you can't be when you are trying to build a website from scratch.

Many people have books that change their life. This can be a religious text, a mindset book or a business book. For me, that book was *Who Not How* by Dan Sullivan. Instead of me asking myself, *How do I do this?* I changed it to, *Who can help me with this?* This was an extraordinary transformation as I was spending hours and hours trying to learn something that people go to college to study for years to become competent in. I thought that I could design and build my new website from SCRATCH and get away with it.

If you want to learn every single skill required to grow a business, expect yourself to be isolated in a room for days at a time and having very little impact on those that you set out to serve. It is impossible to scale and grow a business entirely on your own skill set – you will need the skill sets of others to grow and have an impact. This is my philosophy when I encounter a problem now, I don't ask *how* I can get around it, I ask *who* can help me get around it. If I could turn back the clock, I would have hired someone right at the start so that my website could be completed in a fraction of the time and with a fraction of the stress involved in it.

With all of this in mind, it will be very easy for you to set realistic goals and meet them much sooner than you can expect. There is a wealth of expertise in this world, I urge you to tap into it whenever and wherever you can. You never know, the *who* that someone else is looking for, may turn out to be you and your expertise! I have this mindset too, for those who wish to make their autism-based non-profit or charity self-sustainable through developing courses or a trading component, the *who* in that situation can be me!

TOP TIPS

1. If you have a lack of peace with your past, make peace and accept it as soon as possible.

   Not accepting who you are will have a ripple effect of consequences for you and absolutely everyone around you. I never accepted the fact that I was autistic, and to try and help me do that as a late teenager or a young man, was a futile task. Whenever I finally listened, sought help, and accepted myself, wonderful things happened. This can happen for you and can form the basis of both your personal growth and business growth.

2. Always recognise your own strengths and squeeze every drop of brilliance out of them.

   It is very easy to get caught up in what you may not be so good at – for me, it is technology and anything that involves electricity. I was born three hundred years too late, but this is okay. I realised that I was always a confident speaker, a logical thinker and provider of counsel and advice. These were things I was always good at and will always use as important leveraging tools.

3. Not everyone will love you or be your friend.

   Sadly, not everyone will be supportive on your rise to where you want to be in life. There will be people who want to cut you down at every opportunity and I would like you to make this promise not only to yourself, but to me – promise you will never be someone that tries to diminish the accomplishments of other people in your sector. Just give your all to serve other people and this will pay dividends for you in the long run.

4. Never forget the reason you started doing what you are doing.

   I started out to make the world a better place for autistic people like me. That was my goal, my passion, and the reason I got out of bed every morning. It can be very easy to get carried away and imagine a life full of exotic Italian cars, private islands and making millions while you sleep. Whilst automation and having your business on autopilot can be good, always keep your feet on the ground. Do not make yourself inaccessible to the very people you wish to serve and make the world a better place for.

5. Always ask *who* not *how*.

   Having an unquenchable thirst for knowledge is a good thing – to broaden your horizons, learn new things and develop a deeper understanding of things you may know little about. However, when it comes to business, constantly learning every single skill needed to run a business is both unrealistic and time consuming. You can rely on the expertise of others to meet your goals much more efficiently and without the additional investments of stress and time.

I know you want to change the world – I do too! We all want to in our own way, but it is always important to stay grounded and present whenever you can. Scaling a business to greater heights is an amazing journey. One filled with excitement and adventure, but never forget the important people who have had your back throughout your journey. The ones who encouraged you to start the business, the ones who consoled you when haters hated and the ones who believed in you every step of the way. Your health and family are your true wealth, not material things that will be auctioned upon your demise because you deserted the people closest to you.

Never be afraid to set goals! Never feel ashamed for being ambitious and never be wary of people waiting in the wings with scissors to cut your Icarus wings. The reason I say never be wary is because if every single person is approached with caution, you may be preventing yourself from moving on to the next level. On your journey of levelling up, please ensure you don't fly too close to the sun either.

JOANNE
McMULLAN

PERSONAL DEVELOPMENT JOURNEY

Live, learn, apply new knowledge, skills or experience, and then live, learn, apply new knowledge, skills or experience – this is the cycle that I would describe as my personal journey. This applies to both my career and my personal life. I believe in the motto that every day is a school day and that there is no end to our personal development journey.

I learned that people are either sinks or radiators in life and my draw has always been towards those radiators and to avoid the sinks that would drain the life out of me with negativity, pull me down or make me be a sink too. This has been a lesson for me throughout the years where I can admit to being very much caught up on what other people thought. I got to the point where I was over-analysing every situation and every conversation to be the worst possible scenario, pleasing other people before myself and doing things I didn't necessarily want to do.

I would feel guilt constantly, my life is pretty hectic being a mum of two, a wife, a daughter, a sister, a leader, an employee and so on. And while all of those things are massively important to me, and I am proud of what I have accomplished, the biggest change for me these past few years is that it is very important to take some time out for myself. Whether that is simply going for a walk with the dog or dinner with the girls, it's important to have time to just be me. It is so easy to get lost in the fog, and what I have learned is to 'choose your guilt' – because you will always feel some guilt.

I was on a business flight to the US and I usually only read business books or work on my laptop during flights, but for this flight, for some reason, I turned on the TV and saw *The Secret*. I had heard about this book by Rhonda Byrne many times and was curious to see what it was all about so I watched the movie. I then couldn't get the movie out of my head for the entire trip, so I decided to buy the book as well as the next book *The Power* and more recently *The Greatest Secret*. All of these books most definitely allowed me to 'lift the veil' these past few years, and really open my eyes and my mind to really understand that – as cheesy as it may sound – love is, in fact, the greatest flex you could ever have. These teachings made me realise that you don't just live once, but also only die once, and that life is too short and precious to worry about what other people think, about impressing others – and that isn't about being selfish, but it's about self-care. I had such a great sense of realisation after reading these books that happiness is so important and to not sweat the small stuff in life.

As I started to practice more of the law of attraction, I found myself seeking out like-minded people, books and other resources that increased my knowledge further on this topic. Another book that I would recommend is *Good Vibes, Good Life* by Vex King. Again, this refers to the law of attraction – similar to Rhonda Byrne's teachings – raising your self-awareness and being fully present when you feel emotions such as anger or stress, acknowledging your emotions in the present time but understanding that you are fully in control of how you respond to them so that you can keep them in check. This has really helped me to deal with negative people or difficult situations and I've learned that the way in which some people may speak, react or behave is a reflection of their own emotions and not mine and that they perhaps do not have the same level of self-awareness. That isn't implying I'm a know-all, or I don't slip sometimes, of course I do, I am only human at the end of the day, but I allow myself to recognise it, forgive myself and then get back on track.

Another book that I recommend reading is *Untamed* by Glennon Doyle. This book was quite the eye-opener for my personal development journey and how I think about parenting, and made me really change my approach. There is a section in the book where Glennon takes her child to get her ears pierced and speaks about what bravery actually means. This particular example really stuck with me, about the power of influence that we have on our children, good or bad.

These books have changed my perspective on what personal development means. I used to only read business books for personal growth, and while I still very much read articles and books about business and personal development, for me, it is more about *me* and not just my job or career. The personal development journey I have been on these past few years has changed who I now spend most of my time with. This wasn't a sudden movement, of course, but I think a more subconsciously intentional one over the past few years, whereby I removed myself from very negative, toxic people that were in my life. I now surround myself with those who are happy for me, who enjoy my company, genuinely care and are interested in me, and who are not toxic – they don't gossip, nor do they do drama.

Perhaps it's an age thing too, but I am no longer a people pleaser and I'm definitely not afraid to say no if I really do not want to do something. I really don't feel the need to make a fake excuse like I definitely would have done a few years back or do it anyway just to 'keep the peace', I now simply say, No, *thank you,* and be honest, but while being sensitive too, of course! It is now really liberating to not worry that if someone gets upset because of my non-compliance or if they gossip about me – it simply doesn't matter as I know I cannot control someone else's emotions and that I can only control my own.

I don't ever compare myself or my situation to anyone else or what they have. I was definitely a victim of this, for sure! However, now, when someone gets a new car or house, for example,

I feel genuinely happy for them accomplishing what they set out to achieve, and then focus only on what I have set out to achieve for myself and my family. This is a refreshing feeling, compared to one of resentment and envy.

I always try to make myself available for my friends if they want to talk or simply have a rant, but instead of listening to respond to them, I now simply listen to understand their perspective and ensure that I ask questions to help them navigate decisions, rather than giving my opinion, even if I have one. I know the difference between true friends – of which there are very few – and the many acquaintances we have in our lives. My grandmother always told me that you could only count your friends on one hand and that was if you were extremely lucky – gosh, how right and wise she was.

TOP TIPS

- Don't let your current situation define your future situation.
- The only ceiling you have is the one you create for yourself.
- Always do more than expected – hard work always pays off.
- Every day is a school day, never stop learning.
- Listen to understand, not just to respond.

AMANDA
SCHUBERT

THE MINDSET OF AN ENTREPRENEUR

For a long time, I didn't consider myself an entrepreneur. Partly because I didn't fully understand what an entrepreneur actually was – in my mind, I visualised businesspeople in fancy suits walking swiftly down a city street with their phone pressed to their ear, negotiating deals and generally doing other very-important-person-type things.

Now, while this isn't as far from the truth as I suspected, I now understand that entrepreneurs come in all forms, all industries, and they can vary from regional business owners to the high-flying experts in their fields. Little did I know, when I was a stay-at-home mother of two looking to make a bit of money, that I would soon be reaching heights I couldn't even dream of at the time. I was an entrepreneur before I even knew what that meant!

Part of what separates entrepreneurs from other workers, employees and staff is their mindset. Ask anyone what they consider 'taking a risk' to mean, and the answers will be incredibly varied. But what seems to be more common amongst the entrepreneurial folk out there is that their mindset around risk-taking tends to be more flexible. Why, though? What kind of mindset 'hacks' contribute to someone seeing the potential for success outweigh the risk of failure?

In my personal experience, I have been driven by the idea that anyone has the potential to thrive under the right circumstances. For some, that means they find their greatest success in working for someone else; those people who fill the vital roles that contribute to a functioning society, taking up the foundational jobs that humanity has come to rely on extensively. These workers are no less valuable than the extraordinary visionaries and leaders who are shaking up the world. But I was never satisfied being one of them.

One of my favourite quotes, which I feature on my vision boards every year, is this one by famous entrepreneur and founder of the Virgin Group, Richard Branson:

'If someone offers you an amazing opportunity and you are not sure you can do it, say yes – then learn how to do it later.'

This is one of my fundamental values and one that I rely on more than any other in my mental toolkit. Many of my greatest successes have come from saying *yes* to opportunities, even when I was unsure if I could make the most of them. It was this mindset that led me to taking the risk of investing in a trip to Ireland to network with authors and publishers, which launched me into my career. But I will touch more on this key moment in later chapters.

My attitude to money has been something I also needed to change in order to pursue my goals. I had a deep-seated fear of lack – of not having enough to get by. This created a fear of spending, but also, paradoxically, instilled this lack of confidence in charging appropriately for my services. As someone who was reluctant to part with my money, I found it difficult to convince others to pay their money to me, even when I deserved it. We pay for goods and services, that is how it goes, right? But my relationship with money prevented me from allowing this exchange to flow, and it was something I had to change.

I now avoid using the word *spend* regarding money. To me, *spending* implied impulsively wasting money on frivolous items. Now, I consider every purchase I make an *investment*. I invest in food to sustain me, I invest in clothing for comfort and to enhance my appearance, I invest in entertainment to support my wellbeing, and so on. I also acknowledge that when people purchase my products and services, they are investing in *me*, and I find this far more motivating than considering people spending money on me, and it also provides me with greater incentive to offer my very best work. After all, if people are investing in me and my time, they believe in what I am doing, and I will repay them by doing the very best I can.

A growth mindset is a key tool for an entrepreneur. The ability to see challenges and setbacks as stepping-stones on a journey is vital – otherwise many would quit the moment things got a little rocky. I'm not going to sit here and pretend everything has always gone to plan, or that I haven't been knocked down a peg or two. But the ability to take the lesson and move forward is vital; that's where a resilient attitude is necessary for growth.

In my entrepreneurial toolkit, I use these three tools on a daily basis:

- Saying yes to opportunity.
- An attitude of abundance and gratitude.
- Fostering resilience through challenges.

The mindset of an entrepreneur utilises all three to succeed. Taking risks, rising to challenges, and seeing every moment as an opportunity to grow gives me the courage to try something new and to not limit myself; in this day and age, with technology allowing us to connect with people all over the world, there are truly no limitations to what we could achieve. All we need is the belief that we *can*.

PERSONAL DEVELOPMENT JOURNEY

As a child, my self-esteem was extremely low. I was quiet, shy and kept to myself. Bullies found me an easy target, while, to the others, I kind of blended into the background. Always just kind of *there*, without contributing much. I had little drive or motivation to pursue a career or any line of study once high school was over. University courses didn't interest me, and I had no desire to place all my eggs in one basket, so to speak. As in, I felt reluctant to keyhole myself into a single career path. Even then, I preferred working for myself, doing my own thing. This would later form the foundation for my foray into self-employment, and ultimately, entrepreneurship.

Over the years, I worked many jobs. Hospitality, customer service, domestic service … if it paid money, I did it. But I was unhappy. I felt restricted working for others, following their schedules and rosters. There was only one option for me – I needed to become my own boss. So, I looked at other options for self-employment, something where I could spend my days doing work that I loved. After all, if you love your job, you'll never work a day in your life, right? Something I did enjoy was learning how to create things for myself, things that brought me joy. Artwork, writing stories for myself, and eventually, learning how to make soy candles. I figured why buy them when I could make my own?

Running my own business was mentally and emotionally satisfying, but financially, I still had a fear-based mindset around money. I struggled to justify my prices to myself and fell into the trap of underselling myself and my products. When I transitioned out of making candles into selling my art, the same problem followed. After advertising my work on social media, I was offered an opportunity to illustrate a children's book for White Light Publishing House. Taking into consideration the wise words of Richard Branson, I did exactly what he said: I said yes, then learned how to do it afterwards.

As so often happens when we are working in alignment with our inner knowing, doors began to open all over the place. Through White Light Publishing, I connected with Karen McDermott and Serenity Press. Following Serenity Press on social media, an opportunity came up to travel to Ireland for a writer's retreat. Ireland had long been on my list of places to visit, and I was so excited to see this chance. However, the timing was not right for me then. I wanted to write a book, but had not actively started, and I was still working on adapting my mindset to that of an entrepreneur. So, I let it pass.

Our intuition is a marvellous thing. Seeing that opportunity lit a fire in me, and I set about working on a novel. I knew that the inaugural retreat was not meant for me, but I had that inner knowing that I would have my chance. The following year, it came around again, but was being held in Western Australia. Once more, I let it pass – I needed to be in Ireland. This was not the opportunity I was being drawn to. Instead, I did something very unlike me – I returned to life as an employee. I put my own business on the backburner for the time being, throwing myself back into the workforce. I knew it was necessary in order to grow, but I'd be lying if I said it was easy!

Over the next year, I worked hard to save up my money. I was certain that the opportunity I was waiting for was coming, and I wanted to be prepared. While I struggled being back in a position where I was working for someone else, I made the sacrifice necessary to pursue the larger goal. It was the *big picture* moment that I was focused on. Resilience came to the fore here; without the determination to push through what was a challenging time for me, I would not have been able to take the leap I needed.

Sure enough, the moment I'd been waiting for came around once more. Serenity Press was hosting a writers' retreat at Crom Castle in Ireland in 2019. I didn't hesitate – my name was the first on the list. It was happening. No turning back now. All I needed now was a story I'd written ... *hmm*.

With that goal in mind, I kept working the daily grind while using every spare moment to put together a draft to share with the ladies in Ireland. My plan was to gather as much knowledge and information as I could while on this retreat, to soak up the wealth of experience of those I would be spending the week with. I struggled with imposter syndrome, and with only a month left to go until the retreat, I remember crying to my husband that I was being irrational, leaving him with my two young children to fly to the other side of the world, with nothing more than a half-written first draft of a novel. Who would take a risk like that?

Thankfully, he had more faith in me that I did at the time. I got on that plane, setting myself the goal of getting feedback and advice on how to proceed with getting my story published. But my intuition knew what it was doing. The group of ladies I met were exactly the right people for me. Within a few months of the retreat, I had signed a contract with Daisy Lane Publishing for my trilogy of books, with my first novel, *The Bards of Birchtree Hall,* officially releasing thirteen months after the retreat, on 13 November 2020. Since then, I have featured in three more anthologies, and have my second novel due for release in November 2021.

The fire of entrepreneurship had been fuelled, and I have not looked back. From the quiet girl with no motivation, I am now a woman who is determined to make a difference. It is this drive that led to me joining the Inner Circle, having my book placed in the Hollywood swag bag honouring Oscar nominees, and making connections with other entrepreneurs and high-flyers across the globe. I want to be the example to others of what can happen when you have faith in yourself, back yourself and stay true to yourself.

Was being a game changer something I believed would happen when I took the risk to start up my own little candle-making business back in 2015? No. I just knew that I was not destined to follow the crowd and wanted the freedom to work for myself. It has not always been easy, and there are always obstacles to overcome, but I now embrace them all. We cannot grow if we are not challenged. Sometimes the risks don't pay off, but knowledge is born from experience, and resilience fosters courage. I have no intention of slowing down and cannot wait to see what comes next.

BUSINESS ADVICE

I have been self-employed in some form and fashion since 2015. But the business I started back then is not the same business I have now. I have grown and adapted, always looking to expand and move forward. Adaptability is the greatest singular piece of advice I can offer anyone looking to venture in the world of entrepreneurship, and I will keep shouting it from the rooftops.

Adaptability … adaptability … adaptability!

Why? Because that is the way the world operates. We, as a collective, are constantly evolving, changing, adapting and moving with the times. Those who cannot or will not are often lost in the dust.

We are seeing a great change in the structure of the world right now. The age of COVID-19 has *forced* humanity to change, and change fast – virtually overnight, everything we knew was ripped out from under our feet. Borders were closed, lockdowns were slammed on us, and the whole world came to a shuddering halt. Eighteen months later, we are only just beginning to emerge into what will be the 'new normal'. Bleary-eyed, shaken, and many of us feeling like our foundations have crumbled to dust.

Businesses *had* to adapt, or they disintegrated. Livelihoods were taken away, whole careers were decimated and small businesses were trampled under the weight of a collective crisis. Online meetings became the norm – Zoom became a household name, the app company absolutely boomed out of its skin as people shifted to working from home – conducting business via online platforms. Even now, I probably attend a Zoom meeting with colleagues and friends at least once a week. The world was closed, but the online space widened exponentially.

Hospitality businesses had to resort to takeaway options or other food delivery services. Event coordinators had to create virtual platforms to host guests. Everywhere you turned, businesses were changing and creating new ways to operate. The number of personal services who created online programs – yoga sessions from home, online classes, virtual mentoring sessions ... the list is endless.

I adapted – as an author, I was hit less destructively than many others, but I had to host my book launch online. I relied on the likes of Amazon, Booktopia and other online retailers to sell my books. I couldn't take them on tour – I was supposed to return to Ireland and travel the country with my books. But I had to change that plan. I had to pivot and reset, to look into other options. As a business owner, resilience and adaptability became my greatest assets.

My social media presence skyrocketed. To reach a broader audience, I had to find them – and they were all at home, on their computers, tablets or phones. Marketing became an aspect of my business that I had to learn on the fly. Without the option of face-to-face meetings and opportunities to sell my products, I had to learn new skills. I am still learning!

I had used Facebook for many years already, for my various business pages. But I kicked it up a notch, paying for promotions and ads. Instagram had always been a social site for me, and I used it mainly for personal connection. But I created a business page and started reaching out to others in the industry – particularly a subcommunity I discovered known collectively as 'Bookstagram'. These were the people I needed to connect to.

If I had not been open to change, to shifting my mindset from one of panic and despair to one of *what can I do next?* then I would not be achieving the goals I am today. My social media presence led me to Gary Doherty and the Inner Circle, to Celebrity and Hollywood Gifting (who I approached about getting my book into the Hollywood swag bag honouring Oscar nominees, which were gifted to the nominees and winners of the 2021 Oscars), to book reviewers and promotional services in the US and UK, and to many other people who have helped vault me into heights I couldn't have imagined.

Getting stuck in our ways is detrimental on many levels, but particularly for entrepreneurs. The whole nature of being an entrepreneur is to push boundaries, to try new things, and to ask ourselves – and the rest of the world – *Why not?* To take our businesses to the next level, it requires us to adapt. To take every experience and find a way to grow from it; the good, and the bad.

Not every business will make it through COVID-19. It has changed the landscape so dramatically that many people's livelihoods will not cope, and there is no easy solution to fix this. In an era where nothing is certain anymore, it is impossible to say what the future will hold. The only advice I can give is to be flexible, be adaptable. Every day brings new challenges, new uncertainties. Here, we have just come out of yet another lockdown, where businesses who were just beginning to recover were suddenly thrown into disarray again; for many, it has been the last straw.

Be adaptable. Look at new ways of doing things – can you take your services online? Can you offer virtual spaces for your clients? Can you transfer skills to another industry – marketing, web design, coaching? Take a risk. Try something different, make yourself stand out. The world is looking for innovators, people to lead the way into the new business landscape ...

Could that be you?

OVERCOMING ADVERSITY

Much like I mentioned in the previous section, overcoming adversity is a mainstay of anyone in business – from world leaders to the local deli owner, everyone has challenges and problems to overcome. This has certainly been taken to the extreme during the COVID-19 crisis. Adversity comes in many shapes and forms, each unique to the individual business and industry. Mindset plays a large role in how we handle these, and taking practical steps can help alleviate some of this stress.

So, let's look at some of the non-COVID-19 struggles for a moment. Even without the trauma of that whole crisis, there are the everyday challenges we as businesspeople have to deal with. Employees, wages, OHS, regulations, handling complaints ... the list goes on. Then there are things like product recalls, defamation suits, dealing with trolls online ... man, does it ever end?

Adversity will hit everyone at some point or another, in some way, shape or form. It is an unavoidable aspect of life in general, let alone in business. But how do we overcome it? What strategies can we have in place to help us navigate our way out when things get a little rocky?

For me, personally, one of the biggest challenges I have faced in my business is location. I live in a rural community in South Australia. We are three hours away from Adelaide (our capital city) and eight hours from Melbourne. Honestly, it takes the same amount time for me to drive to Mildura Airport and fly to Melbourne than it does to drive to Adelaide! As a result, I don't get to the city often. Which means many opportunities often take great sacrifices to achieve. For example, attending a business function in the city may be easy enough for those who live there. But, for me, it means long travel, usually an overnight stay, and I potentially lose two days of work for what may be a two-hour conference.

In order to overcome the limitations of my living circumstances, I've had to be creative with marketing and delivering my services. Online platforms have become a vital part of my success. Attending meetings via apps like Zoom and utilising social media to connect and collaborate with others has become a staple of my daily routine. The nature of my work means the majority of it can be done on the laptop at my kitchen table!

I do miss being able to meet with people in person, though. Being able to see people, to speak about my stories, to meet fans and sign books for them – these are all luxuries now, rather than the norm. But I have adapted as best I can to make my situation work for me. Through getting creative and looking into other ways to interact with others, I now have a lot of international connections that I value highly, as well as other connections across Australia. I couldn't give up just because I couldn't travel; I had to be resilient and keep pushing forward.

The more we learn about the power of the mind and how it affects everything in our lives, the more we understand what separates those who thrive through adversity, and those who crumble under it. One of my favourite little sayings, which my husband and I have adopted as a semi-motto for our family is, 'We'll make it work.' Whatever life throws at us, we make it work for us. If we need money, we find ways to earn it. We look into loans, we adjust our budget, we swallow our pride if we have to. Whatever it takes to get back on our feet. When I wanted to get to Ireland, we made sacrifices and we changed our lifestyle to make it happen. Whatever our circumstances, we never lose sight of what we want to achieve, and we do what it takes to get there.

Having a mindset like that, where we see the bigger picture at all times, makes the tough times bearable. Sometimes we have to make short-term sacrifices to achieve the long-term goals. Asking for help when we need it, taking advice from those who have more experience, utilising every available option rather than stubbornly refusing to change our ways is what has led us through every stage of our life. For seven years, I was a stay-at-home mother. We dropped back to one income because we wanted to have one of us home with the children until they started school. It meant a lot of luxuries we had grown accustomed to had to go. Our way of life changed, but it was important to us to be there while the kids were young. We made it work.

Adversity shows us more about what we value than we realise. When the times get tough, it very quickly becomes apparent what matters the most. What are the first things we sacrifice? In business, what are the priorities? What do you refuse to let go of, and what do you allow to fall away? Once we know what we value, the way forward often becomes clearer. When I had my daughter, I tried to return to work. But I very quickly found my mental health deteriorating. The extra income was great, but I was struggling with working when I wanted to be home with my baby. I valued my time with her more than having more money. I knew, then, what had to go.

Overcoming adversity requires us to really understand what we hope to achieve from our business, then taking the steps to make it happen. When things go wrong, our mental toolkit becomes our most valuable asset. Can we adapt? Do we change our approach? What is working, and what isn't? Do we keep pushing through, or do we pivot and move in a new direction? Every answer will be as unique as the individual going through it. But having a clear idea of your goals, your values, and your coping strategies will be invaluable.

As with any aspect of life, when things get tough, our true colours shine through. Do we blame others, give up, and react with anger or aggression? Or do we dig deep, adapt and grow, and embody the true spirit of resilience?

I know which one I choose.

GOALS & GOAL SETTING

I LOVE setting goals. I am mad for it. One of the first things I do in the morning at work is get out my journal and plan goals. Daily, weekly, monthly, long-term – I am constantly looking to where I want to go, while keeping an open mind. After all, plans change – life changes. Being adaptable means learning to adjust on the fly. But having goals reminds us why we're doing what we're doing. Even if we don't tick every single one off the list, it gets us in the mindset of growth. Which is never a wasted day!

As I now look at all my purchases as investments, so do I look at my time. What do I want to invest my valuable hours in? Where is my time best spent in any given moment? How will this investment pay off in the future? These are things I ask myself on a daily basis, sometimes from moment to moment. One of the most common things I get asked by people when I tell them what I do is: 'How do you find the time?' I don't have any more hours in my day than anyone else does. Twenty-four is the maximum. Sleep is non-negotiable, so that is always on there somewhere. But the rest of the hours in my day are *mine*. Only I can decide how I'm going to spend them. So, how do I set goals to make the most of this precious resource?

I have long-term goals. I don't put a time limit on them, like a 'five-year plan' or 'by the time I'm fifty I will have …' because, let's face it – life happens. COVID-19, anyone?

Rather than cage myself into deadlines and *must-do* timelines,

I take a more fluid approach. I always knew I was going to write a book, for example. I didn't know if I'd be twenty or eighty-five. But I was going to do it. So, I made choices that supported that goal. I worked on stories; I made time to write ideas in notebooks, to jot potential plot lines on whatever piece of paper I had within reach. Many of them will never get further than that. But each little snippet that I wrote down reminded me of what I wanted to achieve.

I have always wanted to build my own home. I would frequently search for land for sale in our area, even if we weren't actively looking to buy at that time, just to keep an eye on what was around. That way, when the perfect plot of land came up, I had a clear vision of what I wanted, and put the wheels in motion to purchase it. We bought our plot of land within two months of seeing it for sale.

Some days, my goals are less far-reaching. Because, at the end of the day, I am human. I get sick. I get exhausted. My mental health reaches breaking point and I need to stop. But I do not see these as wasted time. I invest in my health so that I can come back stronger. I invest my time into healing so that I can keep going. Because if I push myself through it, I will lose far more time in recovery than if I had only stopped when it first started to niggle at me. I do not resent my mental health days. I do not feel guilty for putting the brakes on and just resting when I need to. Because I serve no-one when I am empty, when I am floundering. My family suffers, my business suffers, and I suffer when I don't take regular breaks.

One day my goal may be to make sure I drink water and have at least one decent nap. Other days, I have back-to-back Zoom meetings, interviews or social media posts to organise. I do not stick to a rigid schedule. But I never lose sight of my goals, either. Those values I mentioned earlier? They drive me in every goal

I set. I want freedom, I want to inspire others to follow their dreams, and I want my words to reach the world. These are my *big three* – the overarching goals that I hope to achieve in this lifetime. And every little step I take is leading me to them.

For many years, I was aimless. I had no idea what I wanted to do. We are asked as children, 'What do you want to do when you grow up?' I don't like that question. First of all, when do we 'grow up'? Is it at thirty? Is it seventy? When? When is that deadline? If I have a career at twenty-five, does that mean I can't try something new at forty? Rather than asking children what they want to be when the grow up, what if we ask them what makes them happy? What do they love doing, what are they not so interested in? Because, believe me, as an adult, I'm still asking myself these things!

It is only once I let go of the idea that I *had* to be something that I truly felt like I had a goal. Ironic, huh? Once I knew that my ultimate goal was to love my life, then everything else became clearer. My goal was to run my own business. To become an author. To have the freedom to work for myself.

Like a tree sending out new branches, my goals have grown from the trunk of that ultimate goal. Now, through the connections I have made, I have new goals. I want to produce a TED Talk. I want to see my books adapted for the big screen. I want to connect with people across the globe. I want to encourage children to use their unique talents, their unique voices. With every goal I reach, new branches form. It is a beautiful cycle. Every day, I am investing my time into my goals. I am making conscious choices in every moment to do what is in my best interests. Because when I am at my best, I am serving those around me with the best version of myself and what I have to offer.

My time is limited. One day, I won't have any more left. That's a fact. So, while I have it, I'm going to use it. I'm going to work at achieving what I want to do with my life. I no longer spend it mindlessly on things that do not serve my best interests, nor do I give it away just to please others. I have learned to say *no* to things that do not resonate with me, or that no longer serve me. My goals are important, and I invest in them every day, wholeheartedly. Even the little ones – they all add up to the big picture.

TOP TIPS

- Get to know yourself and what you want to achieve in this life.

    What are your values? What is important to you? When your time is done, how do you want your life to have been spent? Keep the *ultimate goal* broad – this is the trunk of your life-tree; it is from this that all the smaller branches will grow. If your goal is to be happy, start growing the branches that bring you joy and chop off any that do not. Without this foundation, it becomes harder to work towards what you want.

- Stock your mental toolkit with valuable tools.

    Resilience, adaptability, courage and gratitude. I cannot stress how important these tools are when levelling up. Without courage, it is so much harder to take risks, or say yes to opportunities when they arise. Without resilience, every challenge or problem that arises will just drag you down. Without adaptability, the risk of being left behind or collapsing when things change becomes overwhelming. And without gratitude, it is impossible to appreciate how far you have come and how much you have achieved already, or to properly thank those who have helped you along the way.

- Connection is key.

    Over the course of history, humanity has thrived because, at the end of the day, we are social creatures. The first to use tools showed the others, and they learned. They grew. It is as true today as it was back then. We learn through collaboration and connection with one another – for better or worse. We either learn what to do to succeed, or we learn what not to do. Experience and knowledge go hand in hand, and by working together and connecting with others, we gather both. If you want to level up, surround yourself with those who share your vision.

- Don't be afraid to start over.

 Believe me, I know the feeling – when you've invested so much time and energy (and often money!) into something, only to realise that it's no longer working for you. The desire to keep forcing it can be strong, because we don't want to let go, or because we hate the idea of 'failure'. But starting over can often be the absolute best choice we ever make. The captain going down with the ship is an outdated philosophy. If it is no longer working, either adapt it until it does, or let it go and start over. Have the courage to recognise that your time is better spent elsewhere, and move on.

- Your time is an investment – use it wisely.

 There are twenty-four hours in a day. Basic survival needs include sleep, food and water, and physical activity. Once they are satisfied, look at how many hours you have left. Chances are there's quite a few. Now, what are you going to invest them in? Family? Work? Leisure activities? The choice is yours, and everyone will have different priorities. And they will change from day to day, from hour to hour. If you want to level up, decide what your time is worth to you, then invest it wisely. Don't waste it frivolously, or give it to someone or something that does not serve your best interests. One day, it will be gone. How you spend it will be up to you. Make it worth it.

NINA
AOUILK

I have been an entrepreneur for the past twenty-eight years. *What makes you want the life of an entrepreneur? What would your personal reasons be? How do you find the will and effort needed to create a business?*

Shall we start at the beginning? In this chapter I will take you on my journey as I unknowingly became an entrepreneur at the age of twenty-three by looking for an opportunity to earn. A young mother, living in rented accommodation with a partner who had little ambition nor concern to provide. The fuel to my fire was that I wanted to give my daughter everything I had never had. She was my motivation to succeed and to break the restrictive chains of what I had believed I was capable of in my career. The programming cycle from culture and parenting from which I had still to discover my personal power and ability to succeed.

I started selling mobile phones in 1993 as they had just become available to buy for domestic use, with a small handset cost and a monthly contract. Living in a small town above a newsagents shop with a four-month-old baby, I was desperately looking to find something that would create the lifestyle I yearned to provide for my baby daughter. I spent a lot of time in the newsagents looking for company and human interaction. I knew most of the locals but every now and then the newsagent shop would serve a stranger, and often they were the ones of interest.

Late one Monday evening, I stood listening to a customer chatting with the shop owner. When he left, I dashed after him to ask him if I could work for him. He stood beside his new shiny black BMW, dressed in a gingham shirt and dark blue jeans, smiling. He explained that he was a distributor for mobile phones, earlier in the newsagents he had been bragging that he was making 'easy money' by signing people up to contracts, gaining healthy commissions and charging them for the mobile handset as well. He called it a win-win situation and mentioned that he was unable to serve all of the customers that contacted him as he simply could not meet the demand.

He commended my courage to jump into things I knew little about and drove away smugly. I felt disheartened as I watched his car disappear around the corner but also felt challenged and understood that I needed to do something more to prove to him that I was serious about taking on the role of a sub-distributor that I had created in my head. We didn't have Google in those times, so I took to scanning through a heavy, dusty *Yellow Pages* directory to find his details. I ran my finger down the business pages feeling defeated as I was unaware of the company name nor his full name – all I had was the city from which he worked.

I decided to pay for the use of the telephone 192 service where I could ask a telephone operator for help. I did not have a telephone in my flat, so I rushed to the nearest red telephone box. It got darker and darker as I prised the heavy door open with the pushchair as my daughter slept snuggly wrapped to protect her from the cold. The telephone service provided contact details of registered individuals and company contact numbers from a directory. The advisor found him within minutes, since the mobile phone industry was very new there were only two businesses registered within the Kettering area. I carefully wrote down the company name and address. There was a spring in my step as I pushed my daughter in her pushchair, imagining that I would soon be driving her around in a car instead of in a second-hand pushchair. I imagined living in a house with a garden and white picket fence, and smiled to myself.

When I arrived home, I wrote out a proposal in which I created an agreement that would be a benefit to the owner and myself. I highlighted all the advantages of having a sub-distributor using the foot traffic from the newsagents shop as a customer base and offered to take on any extra interest that he was turning away, providing him with an extra source of income and expanding his stature within the mobile phone industry.

Within a month I had converted one of the bedrooms in my flat into an office with pop-up banners in the landing separating the home life from the new set-up with the marketing material I received. With my passion and drive I was unknowlingly en route to being offered my own dealership direct with Orange (now known as EE), and earning the respect of the very man who had originally taken me as a joke!

I showed initiative and it worked! This was the start of my entrepreneurial journey and that one decision to not accept defeat meant I would go from strength to strength.

Moral of the story being that to be successful you must think ahead of the obvious and spot a great opportunity that can grow as you do.

Within three years I rented a premises and opened up a mobile phone shop in the town centre. Keeping my personal life in balance, I saved enough money to use as a deposit on a three-bedroom house in a nice area of town, overlooking fields, and that had potential for an extension. It had that white picket fence and garden, and my daughter loved it!

I took my daughter to work with me, trying to keep her close, but soon learned the benefits of delegating and finding child care. I had no family or friends so I looked to outsource a solution.

I decided to enrol her into a nursery out of my budget. The other children in the nursery belonged to the local GPs, solicitors and other respected professionals. Spending more than I could budget on nursery costs made me work harder as I knew I had made a commitment. I had learned early on that your network is your *net worth*. I knew that the people around you influence you, so I carefully started my daughter's social learning from an early age. I would often time myself to collect her from nursery at the same time as the other parents, so that I could network with them, inviting them to visit my new place of work for a coffee and then use that time to get to know their needs.

I learned how to tailor my pitch to the needs of the customer, and this is a practice I carried throughout my career. The ability to listen to the requirements of each individual enables you to cater to their needs. Selling to a need, meeting the demand, is a more authentic and honourable way to sell.

The shop that I had rented in the centre of town created a validity to my brand, and I connected with the landlord shortly after a year of renting, asking whether he would sell me the property. I bought the property from him shortly after in a new company name, renting to my existing mobile phone company, separating the business interests, and thinking smart – enabling the profits to be maximised within each entity.

Having a vision and ability to look at business decisions from every possible perspective enables you to make the decisions that are best for your company. Brainstorming within a group is fantastic, as often people will see things that you may be missing, and you can avoid missing the opportunity to take your business in a direction to grow to its maximum. Separating your emotions from business is also important at this stage of growth.

Once I had secured one property, I sought to extend my portfolio to purchase the two properties next door as I had envisaged owning the whole street! It seems ambitious, but I had already put a plan into action as at one point I owned all the properties from number two all the way to number ten.

I bought my second commercial property in the year 2000 when I was thirty years old. It was a significant building next to my own and held a great bearing in the town as it was the original post office dating back to the 1900s. The post office had closed down and the agent was struggling to sell the pigeon-infested building. After a few months I asked to meet with the agent and offered him a subsided rental offer with the option to buy at the price that it was advertised a year later.

The mobile phone business was no longer as busy because the market had become saturated. I had taken on the supply and build of personal computer towers offering additional servicing and maintenance for local companies who used PCs, as I saw the market was under-represented.

I started selling large plasma flat screens and looked for niche high-end products such as bathroom LCD screens as the clientele within the area were well-to-do and they enjoyed modern gadgets – as did I.

As I took on the rental property next door, I was offered a franchise for Tandy, which was a supplier selling electrical parts and gadgets that attracted a new customer base. Staffing was never easy and became a problem as they were not self-starters, and as my family grew, I employed a nanny who provided full-time care for my two younger sons – again elevating my standing within the community and attracting a richer audience who also employed nannies.

The way you are seen to run your business is watched by potential customers and suppliers. The truth was that I had changed direction to suit my customers' needs, but not necessarily by choice. I had employed a nanny as she was more cost effective than paying for two full-time places at a nursery and after-school child care for my daughter. Playing the part of how you are presented is a huge element of success, as again the validation is set in place.

Running two shops now meant that I was juggling staff wages between the two and I had calculated that both shops needed to meet a gross target to stay afloat. Knowing your finances is imperative so that you do not overspend and can push forward to stay in profit. Working long hours and staying busy is pointless if you are only making ends meet and keeping your head above water.

It seems an obvious statement but the whole point of running your own business is to make a profit and understand the value of your own time. You need the ability to be flexible for change and to reinvent your business should you notice that the trends of what services and products you are providing begins to decline. If you find that you are not enjoying the line of work you are in, then take steps to reinvent your brand and stay interested because your enthusiasm is a huge part of whether the end user uses your services and returns, recommends and rebuys from you.

Spend time with each division of your company even if you are a small set-up – it is necessary to understand how each department is working, to brainstorm or think about what needs to be improved. Constructive criticism is more valuable than positive feedback as you can improve knowing where the business needs work.

Creating a firm and fair relationship with staff is crucial as they are essential parts of the puzzle so that when the team comes together it is a natural organic unit who reflect onto those that become your clients and customers with a united, consistent message.

Having the staff all sing from the same hymn sheet will capture the customer's trust and returning business is more likely, as the way you make people feel reflects upon their choice of where they are willing to spend their hard-earned money.

At this stage in my career, I had established a noticeable standing just off the town's high street and this gave new clients and customers confidence that my business was a reputable expanding company who was able to provide solutions to their needs.

Trust is not an easy thing to attain but it is an asset and unique selling point within itself. Once people have good experiences with you on a professional level, they will buy whatever product you are selling as they have built up a good connection.

The franchise that I had bought into folded abruptly which left me unable to restock items, so I took to sourcing another project and rented out the commercial properties to tenants. Being self-employed requires the ability to not dwell on any failures, the instability of market requirements and your marriage to franchise chains. It was only a matter of time before I had cleared the leftover stock from the franchise and proceeded to rent out both commercial properties, having purchased them, which created a consistent additional source of income. With the rent paid to me over a decade I was able to consolidate all mortgage loans and pay them off, giving me a mortgage-free enterprise.

Always look at ways to maximise profits and the easiest way to create an additional residual income source.

Life is a long learning journey. The lesson that I learned was that you need to know when it is time to accept that one chapter in your career is over and find an alternative way to create revenue. The art of reinvention is used by people in the public eye for the purpose of keeping their audiences engaged. With a business mindset you must be open to change and to accommodate new challenges. Learning how to not be emotionally attached to elements of the business is key, as a successful business is ever changing and growing.

With both commercial properties rented out I had more flexibility to spend time with my family which created a healthier life balance. I decided to follow a career that continually presented itself to me which was in the field of fashion. I started using a small office in the rear of my building and started to forecast fashion colours. I taught myself to spot the trends of colours and the rotations, and with this I would approach local manufacturing companies to offer them my services.

Factories were supplying garments to all the main high street fashion stores. I would watch the representatives come into the factories with their job brief and to place orders that were in excess of a thousand garments. By having my ears and eyes open, I soon learned that there was more of an earning opportunity than the one that I had tapped into.

The way in which you present yourself is received within the first eight seconds. Most of my clients were men and they respected me because I respected myself. My personal relationships had affected my choice of acceptable attire, which helped me as I was always well presented and received as an expert in my field by the way I looked and the confidence in which I delivered myself.

I would assess the needs of a company before I spoke about the products I could supply, this helped to encourage sales as I was fulfilling the customers' needs. It sounds like common sense but you do not benefit trying to sell a product to an end user who has no need for it.

Having given colour forecasts to the customer, I decided to sell fabric of that colour in large quantities by ordering the fabric from Asia by the container-load. I traded on a money up-front basis with urgency as the tool to secure the order as colours changed from season to season, and often customers did not want to be left with surplus stock of fabric nor to miss out.

I would help the factory owners to sell the end garments by hanging around their factories so that when the store representatives visited I could engage in a conversation. I later acted as the go-between for the stores and charged them accordingly. I speak several languages which ensured that the finished garments were made exactly to the specifications as required by the stores.

I had grown from supplying knowledge to providing services but I knew there was more that I could do. As I was growing I moved the new business into an industrial park near the children's school so that the commute would be shorter and so that I had more space to spread out and grow.

Most of my customer base were screen printers. I started to research the developing film they used which allowed an image to be transferred onto a screen plate with which they printed the designs onto a garment. Within two months I became the sole UK supplier of transfer film from a reputable company based in the Netherlands. Again, I was in a market that had few competitors so charged a higher price and was able to supply the product without giving credit nationwide.

This was a prosperous part of my journey until the market became saturated. My partner at the time introduced a gentleman who came onboard as a technical director. This gentleman went on to empty the company bank account and absconded with over £65,000 of money that belonged to the company. Take heed with whom you allow into your business as wolves are often dressed as sheep.

I bounced back with the little stock I had and I knew that I needed a new direction and product. My hunger to find the next new thing took me to the next venture that I would embark upon. I decided to visit trade shows that showcased the latest technology and new industry products within the production of garments and printing field.

I travelled to the European trade shows with my children, allowing them to enjoy the hotel facilities whilst I networked, researched and made myself known at such events. I was soon recognised by main distributors, and came across a new concept of printing onto garments. This was a great business move as I became the only European supplier for a Brazilian printing machine that pressed ink using heat into a garment – which is known as sublimation.

The unique selling point for this style of garment printing was that it was more durable and long-lasting than the screen-printed T-shirts. The screen-printed items have the ink set and dried upon the garment's surface which cracks and fades over time. The new method created longevity. Prices could be increased, as could profit, because the running costs were similar in comparison to the traditional screen-printing method.

This new sublimation system allowed me to provide training, servicing and continual consumable sales. I just needed to persuade the traditional printers to try something new. Believing in a product is the key to sales so your body language and enthusiasm is organic and not forced. Customers are more likely to buy into a product that you are excited about – and I was!

I set up part of my unit as a showroom with a cheap coffee machine, chairs and printed fabric that I draped across the walls creating a gallery of possible prints.

With the showroom set in place, I invited current customers to my new set-up to entertain them and showcase the new products. Knowing that if one customer bought into the new product it would create a domino effect as the other printers suffered from the fear of missing out. I decided to allow the customer themselves see the benefits, and the invitations were sent out creating an unheard-of event within the industry which created a hype amongst my customers.

The new printing system became the talk of the town, and as the only supplier, I kept prices and profits high. I sold over ten units within two months. The new sublimation systems were sold at £80,000 per unit which was double the cost. I knew it was only a matter of time before the competitors would enter and infiltrate the market with more cost-effective options, hence time was of the essence. I sacrificed my personal time and effort to ensure that my customers' needs were met. It was a small window of opportunity and temporary sacrifices had to be made. I took delivery of one printer at midnight in an unsavoury part of central England with my eighteen-year-old daughter manoeuvring a machine weighing one ton using two pallet trucks as there were no staff available. Entrepreneurship requires you to step in when needed, as ultimately the buck stops with you.

Once the business was set up and running effectively I allowed it to run itself so I could continue with other projects. I held a weekly meeting to listen to and address any issues that had arisen. I moved the business into the same town as my main customer base to encourage walk-in sales. I had established myself within the industry and would often play the part of a listening ear when customers had personal and business matters that were affecting them. Some of us have that energy that allows others to off-load and I soon became the go-to for anything they needed.

I started to employ graphic designers straight from university. There were two reasons for this. The first was that as a university student my daughter was unable to find a part-time job other than bar work which she was pretty bad at, as most students want to be on the other side of the bar – not on the serving side. I decided to contact local universities and offer training schemes to new graphic designers, as my customer base had always complained about not having enough graphic designers, or that they were unable to place products as per the specifications relayed by the fashion stores.

I started to train graphic designers. I employed one experienced graphic designer and gave him the responsibility to continue my work when I was was absent. We would train the new designers on a part-time basis to fit in with their studies. The office became a busy and lively place to be, and I would hold coffee and breakfast mornings to encourage the staff to mingle to create a collective family feeling. The dread that most people have when they get up to go into work was turned around as work became a place of happy people who were a part of a family business. This extended respect and love was effective as everyone gave their best, and I used a firm but fair attitude when required, but most of the time I was relaxed, and I felt that the staff performed better with the environment that I had taken time to create.

When the graphic designers had finished their studies and graduated, I would place them within one of my customers' sites and receive a 12% commission of the agreed annual wage for the placement. I again became the go-to for trained staff which was an enjoyable part of my professional entrepreneur career as watching the growth and opportunity arise for each designer was personally rewarding. Having the graphic designers working within the customers' sites I would have more repeated orders as the graphic designers were the ones who placed orders for consumables and additional items.

I became known within the industry as I had acquired a reputation that validated me. This trust encouraged new fashion brands to contact me which led me to the next stage of my career within the fashion field. I started talking to young people who would come to me with new fashion brand ideas, and often they were not thought through when they pitched to me. I had something they wanted – knowledge, contacts and guiduance to organise their blueprint upon.

I had the insight of which colours would sell. I had facilities to design and print, and by outsourcing, could produce a finished garment ready for shipping. I discovered, by extensive research, that new startups could attain funding from the universities that they attended. There were pockets of government grants, local council grants and independent grants available by application.

Over time I helped several well-known fashion brands get into major stores and find designers that fit into their vision and brand. I negotiated on their behalf with global corporations and allowed them to take full reign of their businesses when the time was right for me to step away.

Despite several businesses of my own up and running – including a signage company, customised car and van wrapping company and with the fashion multi-sided companies – I stepped away, as my personal life forced me to leave everything other than the coat upon my back and my youngest child's hand in mine.

I left behind a seven-bedroom house in the country, the cars, the commercial properties and the businesses that I had built up. I left without a penny, leaving the business account in credit so that the staff could be paid and the businesses could continue to trade.

Homeless and fighting for survival, I carefully considered what my life's purpose really was. With my son relying on me for financial and maternal support I was motivated to keep going, knowing that he and my other children were reliant upon me.

To cut a long story short, I was taken in by one of earth's angels who allowed me to stay a month in her home. This Christian, loving woman allowed me to focus on earning money so I could re-establish myself and start again.

During the month she gave us shelter, I worked as a packer for £4 an hour in the same factories that I had exchanged thousand-pound deals with shortly before. I helped people with their bookkeeping for minimal costs, I cleaned houses so that my target could be reached to allow me to start again.

There can be no ego when it comes to survival.

I searched deep for my *why*. My *why* was never in fashion or printing or franchises, it was in people. I had a gift connecting and understanding people. I had a gift in helping people to excel, to let go of their inner critics, and to help them to let go of their self-sabotaging habits. I understood that with the relationships that I had built with others that they always felt loved and heard. They felt seen and understood, and I left them with the belief in themselves to start a new brand or make a change within their workplace that would open new opportunities and bring them wealth.

Visiting my daughter in London, I attracted elite well-known athletes who instantly connected with me, leading to hours of exchanging confidential information and feelings that they shared to receive guidance and understanding. I was flown to France, I had a visitor from the US, and soon I found a new opportunity that left me with a sense of 'job satisfaction'. *Could this be my new career knocking at my door?*

Had the universe led me to the point upon which I was supposed to stand? Was this the stage upon which I was destined to share my struggles to help others with their own life journey? My past horrific, unspoken trauma was gifted as a school of education preparing me for my real success.

The whole purpose of my life, career and direction fell into place two years ago. I oozed with an awakening of self-love and acceptance.

I had a choice to find a well-paid job or to follow my dreams of writing a book. To follow my dreams to inspire and motivate those who were most in need. I wrote the book that I always spoke about. *Master Your Life: Live the Life of Your Dreams!* The book that is packed with how to excel quicker using my knowledge from over the years, referencing money, love, self-love, family and health! It has an extra chapter with regards to coping with COVID-19 and keeping up-to-date with today's ever-changing world.

I stood on the TEDx stage and spoke from the depth of my heart, as I live my new life as an activist speaking out against honour killings and human trafficking. I speak out about mental health and domestic abuse. These difficult subjects being my motivation to speak out breaking old comfort zones with the belief that I can and will change laws to save lives. Working on my non-profit endhonourkillings.org to make a start to stop the cultural crimes and injustices that exist worldwide.

I found my niche, coaching the elite across the world, teaching them how to release themselves of the prisons of their past in which they stood, not accepting their successes and fearing the inability to trust in a fast-moving and often surreal environment. I offer them a confidential sanctuary guiding them to find their unleashed personal power and magnetic mindset.

I learned and grew into my traumas and turned them into triumphs, enabling others to find the best version of themselves. This is the stage upon which I choose to stand. I have found my home and with that I am unstoppable as my success is based upon love. The love for what I do and what I stand for. Could you think of a better place to start a new beginning?

TOP TIPS

- Plan, plan, plan. Write down your intentions. This list gives you a step-by-step plan to follow that will lead you to your goals.
- Create an alleviating and supportive network. Choose who is in your circle wisely. In my experience, when I let go of the wrong people, the right ones came into my life. Have a support circle that helps you level up!
- Celebrate small wins. Start to acknowledge every small win that has aligned with your vision. It's the small wins that equate to the larger goals.
- Break up big tasks into small chunks. It can be overwhelming when you have so much to do. Where do you start? Ask yourself what you can do to bring you a step closer to achieving your ultimate goals.
- Get an accountability partner. This is an empowering way to get things done. Acknowledge that you will also help the other person stay in line with their goals.

This high-level global inner circle mastermind group is a peer-to-peer mentoring group used to help members solve their problems with input and advice from the other group members. The concept was coined in 1925 by author Napoleon Hill in his book *The Law of Success*, and described in more detail in his 1937 book *Think and Grow Rich*.

Having a serving mentality is one of the main characteristics we look for from applicants. A serving mentality serves everyone … including you!

We are very proud that we have one of the world's most dynamic and exclusive mastermind inner circles with members from all over the world.

Lightning Source UK Ltd.
Milton Keynes UK
UKHW010639200422
401787UK00003B/239